T0330077

The Profits and Perils of Passion in
Entrepreneurship

ENTREPRENEURSHIP FOOTPRINTS

Series Editor: Per Davidsson, *Director & Talbot Family Foundation Chair in Entrepreneurship, Australian Centre for Entrepreneurship Research (ACE) | QUT Business School (Management), Australia*

Presenting a new series of short books defining the future of entrepreneurship research. Leading thinkers are given the space to build on their contribution to entrepreneurship to give the reader a concise, innovative and 'must-read, must-cite' take on entrepreneurship research.

More in depth than a journal article, shorter than a standard book and refreshing to read, these books will be the starting point for future research in a particular sub-field for both new and established academics.

Titles in the series include:

Entrepreneurial Ecosystems
Theory, Practice and Futures
Ben Spigel

The Profits and Perils of Passion in Entrepreneurship
Stoking the Fires and Banking the Coals
Melissa S. Cardon and Charles Y. Murnieks

The Profits and Perils of Passion in Entrepreneurship

Stoking the Fires and Banking the Coals

Melissa S. Cardon

The University of Tennessee, Knoxville, USA

Charles Y. Murnieks

University of Missouri–Kansas City, USA

ENTREPRENEURSHIP FOOTPRINTS

Cheltenham, UK • Northampton, MA, USA

Published by
Edward Elgar Publishing Limited
The Lypiatts
15 Lansdown Road
Cheltenham
Glos GL50 2JA
UK

Edward Elgar Publishing, Inc.
William Pratt House
9 Dewey Court
Northampton
Massachusetts 01060
USA

A catalogue record for this book
is available from the British Library

Library of Congress Control Number: 2020939098

This book is available electronically in the **Elgar**online
Business subject collection
DOI 10.4337/9781788973403

ISBN 978 1 78897 339 7 (cased)
ISBN 978 1 78897 340 3 (eBook)

Printed and bound in Great Britain by TJ International Ltd, Padstow

Contents

Acknowledgements

Melissa

When Per Davidsson approached me in 2017 to ask me if I wanted to write a book on Entrepreneurial Passion for his new Entrepreneurship Footprints series, I was torn. I had no time to devote to writing a book, especially given the typical lack of career incentives in our field for writing books instead of peer-reviewed journal articles. Yet I also had a strong vested interest in this research stream, having devoted much of my cognitive energies to it since 2002, right after I started my first academic job. And, despite my work on passion representing fewer than half of my publications, this is the stream of work I am best known for, and one I cannot seem to let go of (hmmm, am I passionate about it? Yes!). The bottom line was that I didn't want anyone else to write this book instead of me. I appreciate Per for giving me the opportunity to organize my thoughts on this rapidly growing body of work and to share those thoughts with our community.

I also couldn't think of anyone else I would rather write this book with than Charles "Chuck" Murnieks. Chuck and I have long occupied ourselves at conferences, in e-mails, and on the phone in deep debates and dialogues about the construct of passion both in entrepreneurship and outside of it. While we sometimes approach these conversations from very different perspectives, that has helped us develop a deep and strong understanding of the nuances around passion and how it has been treated in the literature. I am thrilled that Chuck was willing to work on this project with me to share our perspectives on the research that has been done so far, and perhaps more importantly on the substantial work that remains to be done in order to fully understand passion in the context of entrepreneurship and in the field of management. Chuck is not only a collaborator and colleague, but also a friend, and I look forward to seeing what other research mischief we will cause in the years to come!

This project, as well as my entire career, would not have come to fruition if not for the support from and sacrifices made by family. My husband, Jim, has learned more about this topic than any technology engineer would ever want to, and has pushed me to harness and channel my passion for this line of research and to persist in completing projects despite the many obstacles that have been in my path. Our sons, Shamus and Dominick, have been with me for my entire academic career. They have observed first hand how passion alone will not lead to success, but instead you must also invest hard work, dedication, and substantial time spent working toward your goals even when progress is slow (or backwards) and the tasks are mundane. Hopefully they have also seen how my identity as their mom and love for them has been a critical motivation in my career. I truly would not be who I am today without Jim, Shamus, and Dominick, my three boys.

Finally, I would be remiss if I did not thank my entrepreneurial family for the upbringing that led to my interest in understanding them and what drove them. When I was 6 years old my parents founded a business that has profoundly influenced my life, and today my brother and sister are ongoing founders and owners of a wide variety of businesses. What we cannot do, we study, so thank you, Dad, Mom, Bob, and Katherine, for giving me plenty of stories and experiences that I will continue to study in order to better understand. I love you all.

Charles

In 2006, a naïve doctoral student cornered a fiery (passionate) young professor at a conference and proceeded to talk her ear off about her ideas concerning entrepreneurial passion. To his good fortune, she didn't call security to have him hauled away. Rather, she was willing to have one conversation after another about it, which eventually led to a lasting friendship and a kindred interest in this topic. I can't thank Melissa enough for giving me a moment of her time back then, and for being willing to engage in countless hours of subsequent discussion after discussion about the nature of entrepreneurial passion. It has been priceless for me to have someone to bounce ideas off of (both good and bad) and who is as eager to explore the uncharted areas of the passion domain as I am. Collaborations and friendships like this mean more than even the work itself – it's been a true pleasure and an honor.

In this book, we talk repeatedly about how much influence key stakeholders have on individuals and their passions. That's absolutely true in my case as well. My family has provided more love and support than I ever deserved. My wife Deanne often bears the burden of seeing me at my passionate best, and definitely at my passionate worst. She's always there to lend a supportive smile and a welcome ear. She's my best friend. My children, Ginger and Donovan, exemplify passion and excellence in everything they do. I admire their work and revel in simply spending time in their presence. They bring light to any room they enter. In all sincerity, I know that the nature of scholarship often requires our families to sacrifice so that we can sequester ourselves to write and conduct research. My family has never held that against me, and has always been more focused on enjoying our time together, rather than lamenting our time apart. I thank you and love you for that support.

I would be remiss for not mentioning the countless entre-preneurs who have participated in innumerable interviews and surveys to help us understand the nature of entrepreneurial passion. Thank you for taking the time to enlighten us and illuminate this domain. We couldn't conduct this research without your help and your revelatory insights. Lastly, and most importantly, I wish to say thank you to our Lord. My journey as an academic has been richly blessed beyond my imagination, and none of that would have been possible without the condescending grace of my Heavenly Father.

1. Introduction to passion in entrepreneurship

To "stoke" is to poke a fire and fuel it so that it burns higher and hotter. *Stoke* can also mean "incite"; for example, when a surfer says, "I am so stoked," it means she is excited – the fire of her enthusiasm for surfing is burning hotter (vocabulary.com). Stoking a fire can be likened to the experiential phenomenology of passion; passion involves intense feelings for things that are important to you, which can intensify your motivations and emotional reactions so that they burn brighter and hotter. Entrepreneurs are often believed to experience strong passion and to be "fired up" about their products or ventures. Yet, it is difficult for anyone to be constantly excited or to build the fire of their passions ever higher and higher, because at some point exhaustion takes over. Therefore, in addition to stoking a fire, it is also important to be able to "bank the coals." A person banks the coals of a fire when they protect the coals or embers even when the fire dies down to ash. This is done by building a wind screen or covering the coals with rocks, so that there is enough heat in the coals to start a fresh fire in the morning. Banking the coals is also critical for passion. Entrepreneurs may not be able to act with and maintain their intensely hot passion all the time. Yet, they still need to be able to keep a small coal of passion protected so they can reignite their motivation and drive the next day, or later in their career, or with their next venture. This notion of stoking the fires and banking the coals of entrepreneurial passion is the focus of this book, as there are profits to be had but also perils to be avoided in managing and understanding the passion of an entrepreneur by him- or herself, in their team, or as investors or other stakeholders of their firms.

"Passion" is nearly ubiquitous in today's self-help books, company missions, or tag-lines, and in the advice we give to aspiring entrepreneurs. For example, a quick online search reveals that Tropicana is "passionate about juice," Schwan's is "passionate about pizza," Bryan College is "passionate about making college more affordable," and Ellevation Education is "passionate about learning." SnapLogic values "passion to attack difficult challenges," cars.com "infuses passion into everything [they] do," and Sisense is "passionate about the company and its success." River Sports Outfitters' mission for the company and its customers is to "live your passion." Passion is rampant in the mainstream business lexicon.

Similarly, aspiring entrepreneurs are told to "pursue their passion," "grow your creative passion into a full-time gig" (Griffio, 2019), "live your dreams, ignite your passions and run your business from anywhere in the world" (Krieger, 2014), "unleash your inner company: use passion and per-severance to build your ideal business" (Chisholm, 2015), "focus your passions[,] map your direction[, and] build a great company" (Black, 2019), and simply just to "turn your passion into a thriving business" (Gabrielle, 2017) in this twenty-first-century "passion economy" (Davidson, 2020). These are all book titles or subtitles found in seconds on Amazon, where over 1,000 books come up in a search for "entrepreneur" and "passion."

Alongside this rise in practitioner interest in and emphasis on passion, academic research on passion in entrepreneurship has virtually exploded in the last 20 years, with over a 550 percent increase in peer-reviewed publications including the words "entrepreneur" and "passion" from 1999 to 2019. The purpose of this book is to help readers who are new to the world of "passion" for work, and especially entrepreneurial work, to understand the fundamental arguments, agreements, and discrepancies across these bodies of literature in order to better understand the evidence concerning passion, where it comes from, what effects it has, and perhaps more importantly, where the conceptual underpinnings of different perspectives lie. By unpacking different perspectives, as well as commonalities across perspectives, we hope to inform readers so that they can make better decisions about the research they pursue as well as the advice they give to their students and other aspiring and practicing entrepreneurs.

We start by reviewing two fundamentally different perspectives on what passion is, as experienced by individuals. Is passion a motivation or is it a feeling? In Chapter 2 we explore the stream of research and definition put forth by Cardon, Wincent, Singh, and Drnovsek (2009, p. 519) that entrepreneurial passion involves intense positive feelings individuals experience by engaging "in entrepreneurial activities associated with roles that are meaningful and salient to the self-identity of the entrepreneur." We contrast this with a distinctly different yet complementary perspective that passion is a motivation (Vallerand, et al., 2003). Drawing from numerous studies by Robert Vallerand and his colleagues, we unpack the Dualistic Model of Passion (DMP) and its two fundamental constructs of harmonious and obsessive passion, and how this model has been applied to the entrepreneurial context.

While these two conceptualizations of passion are quite different, as the first focuses on the extent to which a person is passionate and the second focuses on the way in which a person internalizes their passion into their identity, they share some important commonalities. For example, passion is experienced for specific targets (e.g., an entrepreneur is passionate about their firm) rather than comprising a personality trait (e.g., an entrepreneur is a passionate person). Passion also involves extremely strong emotions and motivations for targets that are meaningful to one's identity. In addition, passion motivates action toward its target, rather than avoidance behaviors. In discussing different conceptualizations of passion, we are mindful of the fact that there are a number of constructs such as intrinsic motivation and positive affect that are conceptually close to passion. As we discuss in Chapter 2, passion is distinct from these other constructs, but still shares similarities related to its emotional and motivational core. We argue throughout this book that as scholars studying passion, we must be careful and precise in order to conceptually and empirically distinguish and separate passion from these related, but different, constructs.

In Chapter 3, we expand on the fundamental agreements in the literature concerning the core features of passion that we introduce in Chapter 2 – that passion has a specific object and can vary across objects – and that passion involves one's self-identity. More specifically, despite the agreement that the object of passion matters, there are a variety of different objects that can be the focus or source of an entrepreneur's passion, from work in general, a specific career path or occupational identity (e.g., nurse, entrepreneur), specific sub-roles to an occupational identity related to core activities of that identity (e.g., inventing, founding, developing), specific activities themselves (e.g., bike riding, stamp collecting), causes (e.g., a social mission such as providing clean water), or specific entities or other people (e.g., a firm, a founding team, or a family at the core of a family business). We talk about these different targets and existing knowledge about passion for different targets in Chapter 3. We also note that regardless of the target(s) of passion one studies, the object of an entrepreneur's passion must be something that is important and central to the identity of the entrepreneur, as advocated for by both of the primary theoretical perspectives on passion, the DMP and EP (entrepreneurial passion), which we discuss in Chapter 2. We suggest in Chapter 3 and elsewhere throughout this book that studies of "passion" that don't include identity importance are in actuality studies of excitement or enthusiasm, not passion.

In Chapter 4 we shift our discussion to why passion even matters; specifically, we discuss the outcomes in terms of both profits and perils that can result from entrepreneurial passion, which depend both on the type of passion the entrepreneur experiences (e.g., obsessive or harmonious) as well as on the extent of that passion (e.g., how passionate are they about being an entrepreneur, or about specific parts of that career such as being a founder?). As part of that discussion we incorporate not only the entrepreneur's experience of passion but also how the passion they display to entrepreneurial stakeholders impacts potential profits and perils. We argue that displayed passion and/or perceived passion are not the same constructs as experienced passion, and instead suggest that displayed and perceived passion should be examined with labels such as enthusiasm, preparedness, or commitment (Chen, et al., 2009), given that observers cannot readily assess the identity-importance component that is core to mainstream definitions of passion used in entrepreneurship. We discuss important recommendations for how we should carry the study of potential profits and perils of both experienced and displayed passion forward in more conceptually and empirically precise ways.

Given the importance of passion to key outcomes for entrepreneurs, their firms, and other stakeholders, discussed in Chapter 4, we focus Chapter 5 on the antecedents of passion and how we can ignite the fires of passion or stoke its heat through entrepreneurial education, activities, or contagion processes. Here we talk about teaching passion and argue that while educators cannot teach people to be passionate, we can help individuals discover what excites them about entrepreneurship or innovation, and help them understand more of what it means to be an entrepreneur so they can determine if their ideal aspirational identity of "entrepreneur" really aligns with their self-identity in the present or future (Cohen, et al., 2019). For some aspiring entrepreneurs, activity, education, and contagion processes will stoke the fire of passion and make it burn hotter, while for others it may dampen their enthusiasm once they learn what it really takes to be an entrepreneur. This may lead to disengagement from the entrepreneurial aspiration, or may just lead to the small coal or fire of desire for entrepreneurship being banked until later in the individual's career.

In Chapter 6 we expand the focus on individual entrepreneurs to that of entrepreneurial teams. This is important given that teams found over half of all new ventures (Kamm, et al., 1990; Klotz, et al., 2014). We review the very few studies that have been done to date concerning how passion operates within teams, and discuss several areas ripe for additional research. Expanding on this focus on future research in Chapter 7, we suggest other novel areas of study related to passion that have received little or no attention to date in the literature. We revisit methodological issues that need to be considered in order to facilitate more precise investigation of the phenomenon of passion, and make important recommendations for best practices in pursuing these and other future research questions. Finally, in Chapter 8 we briefly share our concluding thoughts on the stream of research to date on entrepreneurial passion, and our hopes for the next generation of work.

Across all of these chapters our intention is not to provide an exhaustive review of all of the research that has been done on passion in entrepreneurship, but rather to elucidate the key arguments and fundamental assumptions of different perspectives on this topic, where there are conceptual similarities, and where these assumptions diverge. This should help readers better understand, compare, and contrast empirical findings from various studies that have used different approaches to conceptualize and measure passion. In Table 1.1, we list the major readings we believe will help readers new to the topic of entrepreneurial passion. This table is not meant to be a comprehensive catalog of all extant work on passion; rather, it suggests a few key readings that provide a good foundation for beginning a scholarly investigation of passion in entrepreneurship.

We hope this book serves to clarify the literature as well as help scholars situate their own approaches and research questions within the growing corpus of knowledge around this topic. In short, we hope to stoke the fires in other academics to study the fascinating questions related to passion for work and entrepreneurship. We also hope to bank some coals of interest that may be uncovered in the future, so that scholars can build anew a resurgence of interest in studying the passion of entrepreneurs and how entrepreneurs can maximize the associated economic and non-economic profits and avoid the potential perils. In so doing, we also hope to "live our passion" in promoting high-quality scholarship and deeper understanding of the phenomenon that has captivated our attention for the past two decades.

Table 1.1   *Key papers on passion and entrepreneurship (organized chronologically within each section)*

Fundamental theory for passion and entrepreneurship (Chapters 2 and 3)

Authors (year)	Type of research	Summary
Vallerand, Blanchard, Mageau, Koestner, Ratelle, Léonard, Gagné, & Marsolais (2003)*	Empirical	The Dualistic Model of Passion (DMP) proposes two types of passion: harmonious (HP) and obsessive (OP). HP promotes healthy adaptation to activity engagement, whereas OP thwarts it by causing negative affect and rigid persistence.
Cardon, Wincent, Singh, & Drnovsek (2009)	Conceptual	Entrepreneurial passion (EP) involves positive intense feelings experienced for activities tied to meaningful and salient role identities. EP promotes opportunity recognition, venture creation, and venture growth by driving certain goal-related cognitions and entrepreneurial behaviors.
Cardon, Glauser, & Murnieks (2017a)	Empirical	Entrepreneurial passion (EP) has numerous different sources/targets, including EP for growth, EP for people, EP for a product or service, EP for inventing, EP for competition, and EP for a social cause.
Cardon, Post, & Forster (2017c)	Conceptual	Entrepreneurial passion (EP) in teams is conceptually distinct from EP within individuals. Both average levels and diversity of individual passions of team members matter, as does team entrepreneurial passion (TEP). TEP reflects the extent and focus of shared intense positive feelings for a collective and central team identity among new venture team members. TEP has a dynamic and cyclical relationship with individual-level entrepreneurial passions, team passion diversity, team processes, team member exits and entries, and venture performance.

Measuring entrepreneurial passion (Chapters 2 and 3)

Authors (year)	Type of research	Summary
Vallerand, Blanchard, Mageau, Koestner, Ratelle, Léonard, Gagné, & Marsolais (2003)	Empirical	The Dualistic Model of Passion (DMP) proposes two types of passion: harmonious (HP) and obsessive (OP). HP promotes healthy adaptation to activity engagement, whereas OP thwarts it by causing negative affect and rigid persistence. A scale for measuring HP and OP is presented.
Cardon, Gregoire, Stevens, & Patel (2013)	Empirical	An entrepreneurial passion (EP) measurement scale is developed and validated. EP is composed of task-specific domains (inventing, founding, developing) that involve (1) intense positive feelings and (2) identity centrality for each domain. EP persists over time.

Intraindividual effects of entrepreneurial passion (Chapter 4)

Authors (year)	Type of research	Summary
Vallerand, Blanchard, Mageau, Koestner, Ratelle, Léonard, Gagné, & Marsolais (2003)*	Empirical	The Dualistic Model of Passion (DMP) proposes two types of passion: harmonious (HP) and obsessive (OP). HP promotes healthy adaptation to activity engagement, whereas OP thwarts it by causing negative affect and rigid persistence.
Cardon, Wincent, Singh, & Drnovsek (2009)	Conceptual	Entrepreneurial passion (EP) involves positive intense feelings experienced for activities tied to meaningful and salient role identities. EP promotes opportunity recognition, venture creation, and venture growth by driving certain goal-related cognitions and entrepreneurial behaviors.

Murnieks, Mosakowski, & Cardon (2014)	Empirical	Entrepreneurial passion rises and falls in association with entrepreneurial identity centrality. Entrepreneurial passion increases entrepreneurial self-efficacy and time spent engaged in entrepreneurial behaviors.
Cardon & Kirk (2015)	Empirical	The relationship between entrepreneurial self-efficacy and persistence is mediated by entrepreneurial passion (EP) for inventing and by EP for founding.
Huyghe, Knockaert, & Obschonka (2016)	Empirical	Higher levels of entrepreneurial passion for inventing (EP-I) predict stronger spin-off and start-up intentions. Obsessive scientific passion is positively associated with spin-off intentions, but negatively associated with start-up intentions. These relationships are mediated by entrepreneurial self-efficacy and affective organizational commitment.
Stenholm & Renko (2016)	Empirical	Entrepreneurial passion for inventing and entrepreneurial passion for developing are each positively related to bricolage. In turn, bricolage is positively related to venture survival.

Firm effects of entrepreneurial passion (Chapter 4)

Authors (year)	Type of research	Summary
Ho & Pollack (2014)	Empirical	Harmonious entrepreneurial passion is related to higher out-degree network centrality, which leads to increased business income, while obsessive entrepreneurial passion is linked to lower in-degree network centrality, which leads to less business income.
Drnovsek, Cardon, & Patel (2016)	Empirical	Entrepreneurial passion for developing (EP-D) is positively related to venture growth. This relationship is partially mediated by goal commitment.
Stenholm & Renko (2016)	Empirical	Entrepreneurial passion for inventing and entrepreneurial passion for developing are each positively related to bricolage. In turn, bricolage is positively related to venture survival.

Mueller, Wolfe, & Syed (2017)	Empirical	Entrepreneurial passion for developing (EP-D) is positively related to venture performance. This relationship is mediated by the entrepreneur's self-regulatory mode (locomotion and assessment) and grit.

Effects of displayed/perceived passion on key stakeholders (e.g., employees, venture investors) (Chapter 4)

Authors (year)	Type of research	Summary
Cardon (2008)	Conceptual	Entrepreneurial passion (EP) can be transferred to employees and other stakeholders through various contagion processes.
Chen, Yao, & Kotha (2009)	Empirical	Decisions to invest in new ventures are driven by the perceived preparedness of the presenter, rather than their displays of passion such as demonstrated enthusiasm.
Breugst, Domurath, Patzelt, & Klaukien (2012)	Empirical	Employee perceptions of an entrepreneur's passion for inventing and developing enhance their affective commitment, while perceptions of the entrepreneur's passion for founding decrease it. Employees' experiences of positive affect at work and goal clarity mediate these relationships.
Mitteness, Sudek, & Cardon (2012)	Empirical	Perceived passion and enthusiasm by angel investors increases evaluations of funding potential. This relationship is moderated by qualities of the investor including age, personality, cognitive style, regulatory focus, and the motivation to mentor.
Murnieks, Cardon, Sudek, White, & Brooks (2016)	Empirical	Perceived passion and tenacity of entrepreneurs increases investment probabilities of angel investors. The presence of both tenacity and entrepreneurial passion is most beneficial. This relationship is moderated by the entrepreneurial experience of the investor.

Cardon, Mitteness, & Sudek (2017b)	Empirical	Preparedness of the presenter positively influences angel investment evaluations, while the influence of enthusiasm of the presenter on evaluations varies. Both relationships are moderated by the specific form of commitment (investment of time, money, and use of funds).
Davis, Hmieleski, Webb, & Coombs (2017)	Empirical	Crowdfunding support is positively related to a product's creativity. This relationship is partially mediated by the prospective funder's level of positive affect. This indirect effect is moderated by the perceived level of passion of the entrepreneur.
Li, Chen, Kotha, & Fisher (2017)	Empirical	Displayed passion by entrepreneurs increases funding and social-media exposure provided by crowdfunders. These relationships are moderated by the perceived innovativeness of the entrepreneur's project.
Warnick, Murnieks, McMullen, & Brooks (2018)	Empirical	Perceived passion for entrepreneurship and passion for a new venture's product/service increase the probability of investment by angels and venture capitalists (VCs). These relationships are moderated by the openness to feedback of the entrepreneur, the type of investor (angel vs. VC), and the investor's experience.
Jachimowicz, To, Agasi, Côté, & Galinsky (2019)	Empirical	Displays of passion increase offers of support to entrepreneurs. Offers of support are partially mediated by status conferral, and moderated by appropriateness, agreement with the target of passion, and the competitiveness of the context.
Oo, Allison, Sahaym, & Juasrikul (2019)	Empirical	User entrepreneurs have greater success at crowdfunding than non-user entrepreneurs. This relationship is partially mediated by perceived passion, product innovativeness, and need similarity with potential funders.

Drivers and sources of entrepreneurial passion (Chapter 5)

Authors (year)	Type of research	Summary
Murnieks, Mosakowski, & Cardon (2014)	Empirical	Entrepreneurial passion (EP) rises and falls in association with entrepreneurial identity centrality. EP increases entrepreneurial self-efficacy and time spent engaged in entrepreneurial behaviors.
Gielnik, Spitzmuller, Schmitt, Klemann, & Frese (2015)	Empirical	Entrepreneurial effort predicts changes in entrepreneurial passion. This relationship is mediated by new venture progress, and moderated by free choice.
Collewaert, Anseel, Crommelinck, De Beuckelaer, & Vermeire (2016)	Empirical	Entrepreneurial passion for founding (EP-F) changes over time. While the identity centrality of EP-F remains stable, intense positive feelings of EP-F decrease over time. The decline in feelings is moderated by venture idea changes, role ambiguity changes, and feedback-seeking behaviors.
Cardon, Glauser, & Murnieks (2017a)	Empirical	Entrepreneurial passion (EP) has numerous different sources/targets, including EP for growth, EP for people, EP for a product or service, EP for inventing, EP for competition, and EP for a social cause.
Gielnik, Uy, Funken, & Bischoff (2017)	Empirical	Entrepreneurship training boosts entrepreneurial self-efficacy and harmonious entrepreneurial passion. Self-efficacy sustains the positive effect of entrepreneurship training on passion over time. The effect of training on business creation is partially mediated by passion over time.
Murnieks, Cardon, & Haynie (2020)	Empirical	Affective interpersonal commitment is positively related to the development of harmonious and obsessive entrepreneurial passion. Entrepreneurial identity centrality drives development of harmonious entrepreneurial passion. These relationships are moderated by gender.

Conceptualization and effects of entrepreneurial passion in teams (Chapter 6)		
Authors (year)	**Type of research**	**Summary**
Cardon, Post, & Forster (2017c)	Conceptual	Team entrepreneurial passion (TEP) is a team-level construct of passion representing the level of shared intense positive feelings for a collective and central team identity for new venture teams. TEP influences individual-level entrepreneurial passions, team member exits and entries, team processes, and venture performance.
Santos & Cardon (2019)	Empirical	Team entrepreneurial passion (TEP) for inventing and developing are positively related to team performance. Monofocal and complete polyfocal TEP are the most beneficial for team performance.
de Mol, Cardon, de Jong, Khapova, & Elfring (in press)	Empirical	In new venture teams, when considered alone, average team passion boosts performance. Yet, when considered alongside team passion diversity, average team passion is not significant, and instead team passion diversity is negatively related to performance. When considering passion among team members, both average levels and diversity of passions must be included.
Boone, Andries, and Clarysse (in press)	Empirical	In order for a team to benefit from experiencing team entrepreneurial passion (TEP), the focus of that TEP should be aligned with the developmental stage the venture is in (conceptualization or commercialization).

Note: * Although this study does not concentrate on entrepreneurial passion specifically, this is considered a foundational paper on passion theory.

2. Passion of entrepreneurs: conceptual underpinnings and distinctions

"Passion" is a loaded word. It has been used in a variety of ways to define a myriad of concepts (Newman, et al., 2019; Vallerand, 2015). While philosophers have studied passion for literally centuries, the examination of passion in psychology and entrepreneurship is relatively new. Across these various bodies of literature, passion has been conceptualized as a feeling, an intellectualized emotion, and a motivation, depending on the author's philosophical orientation.

In the entrepreneurial domain, two primary theories have been employed as the anchors for investigations of passion: the theory of entrepreneurial passion (EP) by Cardon, Wincent, Singh, and Drnovsek (2009), and the Dualistic Model of Passion (DMP) by Vallerand and his colleagues (2015, 2013). Due to the overwhelming amount of work that has grown out of these two primary theories, we discuss each in this chapter. While the conceptualization of EP is, by definition, oriented to the entrepreneurial domain, the DMP was developed in psychology and has been applied more broadly to a variety of work and non-work domains. We acknowledge this breadth and incorporate several important studies using the DMP in contexts outside of entrepreneurship, yet our primary focus remains on studies where the DMP has been utilized in an entrepreneurial context. We briefly review the theoretical underpinnings and bases of each perspective, including areas of overlap and agreement, as well as key differences between these perspectives. We also discuss some other theories and conceptualizations of passion for work and entrepreneurship that have emerged but that are less prominent in the literature.

THE ENTREPRENEURIAL PASSION (EP) CONCEPTUALIZATION

The most prevalent and widely used conceptualization of entrepreneurial passion was developed by Cardon, Wincent, Singh, and Drnovsek (2009). They define entrepreneurial passion as "consciously accessible, intense positive feelings experienced by engagement in entrepreneurial activities associated with roles that are meaningful and salient to the self-identity of the entrepreneur" (p. 519). They argue that entrepreneurial passion results from engagement in activities with identity meaning and salience to the individual. The original conceptualization of entrepreneurial passion by these authors included three distinct entrepreneurial role identities that they argued were particularly salient (based on the literature at that time): (1) an inventor identity involving identifying, inventing, and exploring new opportunities, (2) a founder identity involving establishing ventures and commercializing/ exploiting opportunities, and (3) a developer identity involving nurturing, growing, and expanding ventures after they have been created. Cardon, Glauser, and Murnieks (2017a) have more recently expanded the set of targets for which entrepreneurial passion can be experienced (see Chapter 3).

An important aspect of this conceptualization of entrepreneurial passion is that the feelings of passion an entrepreneur experiences are not for entrepreneurship in general, but rather are for a specific role identity. As such, individuals exhibit entrepreneurial passion for inventing (or for founding or developing) independently, because the passion is directed toward specific activities related to each of these associated role identities. Importantly, an entrepreneur can feel passion for more than one of these role identities, or even all three, but not all entrepreneurs necessarily will. For example, one entrepreneur may be passionate solely for inventing new products or services without interest in the commercialization of those products for sale as a founder, or for scaling that company for high growth. Another founder might be passionate for both founding and growing their firm.

Such configurations that allow for the experience of different levels of passion for different aspects of entrepreneurship are essential components of the EP perspective put forth by Cardon and colleagues (2009). This is because entrepreneurial passion for different targets differentially influences outcomes. For example, entrepreneurial passions for inventing and developing (but not founding) lead to more engagement in bricolage behaviors (Stenholm & Renko, 2016), passions for inventing and founding (but not developing) mediate the relationship between self-efficacy and persistence (Cardon & Kirk, 2015), and perceptions of entrepreneurial passion for inventing and developing enhance employee commitment, while passion for founding hurts it (Breugst, et al., 2012). We expand on these and other studies in Chapter 4.

In general, entrepreneurial passion studied using the EP perspective has found significant ties to consequential outcomes at both the individual and the firm level. For example, empirical studies show that entrepreneurial passion for certain targets drives creativity, persistence, start-up intentions, venture performance, and venture growth (Cardon, et al., 2013; Drnovsek, et al., 2016; Huyghe, et al., 2016; Mueller, et al., 2017).

THE DUALISTIC MODEL OF PASSION (DMP) CONCEPTUALIZATION

The second major conceptualization of passion that has been used in entrepreneurship is the Dualistic Model of Passion (DMP), studied for many years by Robert Vallerand and his colleagues (2015, 2003). Vallerand and collaborators (2015, 2003) define passion as a strong inclination toward a specific object, activity, concept, or person that one loves, highly values, invests time and energy in on a regular basis, and that is part of one's identity. The DMP further differentiates passions into two types based on how the object of passion is internalized into one's identity: harmonious passion and obsessive passion. Harmonious passions emerge from autonomous internalization of an activity into one's identity, which engenders a sense of volition and personal endorsement for the activity (Vallerand, 2015). This produces a strong but controllable desire to engage in the activity because involvement is accepted freely, without contingencies attached to it. Activities related to harmonious passions occupy significant, but not overpowering, spaces within the lives of individuals such that the activities exist in harmony with other identity elements (Vallerand, 2015). In general, harmonious passions lead to adaptive outcomes in an individual's life (Curran, et al., 2015; Vallerand, 2015). For example, studies show that harmonious passion correlates significantly with factors such as positive affect, life satisfaction, vitality, engagement, self-esteem, concentration, and intrinsic motivation, and negatively with outcomes such as negative affect, anxiety, and burnout (Curran, et al., 2015).

In contrast, obsessive passions are defined by controlled internalizations that originate from intrapersonal or interpersonal pressures attached to activities (Vallerand, 2015). These pressures can emerge from contingencies such as an uncontrollable sense of excitement or from the self-esteem attached to activity engagement. Interpersonal peer pressure or feelings associated with social acceptance could also spur the creation of obsessive passions because individuals may feel compelled to engage as a result of the ego affirmation provided (Murnieks, et al., 2020; Vallerand & Verner-Filion, 2013). An individual does not feel the level of autonomy to engage or disengage obsessive passions as they do with harmonious ones, because obsessive passions serve ego protective and defensive functions (Mageau, et al., 2009). Where the ego is involved, it is more difficult to disengage because individuals desire the affirmation provided (Mageau, et al., 2011). As Vallerand (2015) points out, activities related to obsessive passions occupy overwhelming spaces in individuals' identities and may create conflicts with other aspects of their lives. As such, obsessive passions can lead to a mix of both adaptive and maladaptive outcomes (Curran, et al., 2015; Pollack, et al., in press; Vallerand, 2015). For example, obsessive passion has been shown to correlate significantly with identified regulation motivations, negative affect, burnout, and activity/life conflicts. In summary, harmonious passions are engaged freely and autonomously, whereas individuals feel compelled to engage obsessive ones.

COMMONALITIES ACROSS CONCEPTUALIZATIONS

There are a number of important commonalities across these two theoretical perspectives as they relate to the passion of entrepreneurs. First, entrepreneurial passion is directed toward specific objects. Entrepreneurs or founders are not passionate about everything, but rather, are passionate about something specific. As Cardon, Glauser, and Murnieks (2017a) note, that could be an activity, a product, a person, or a mission, but passion must have a target (Cardon, et al., 2009, 2013). Vallerand (2015) is also explicit about this point, emphasizing that numerous philosophers and psychologists agree that individuals are not passionate in general, but are rather passionate about something specific. It is important for scholars new to this field to know that across conceptualizations and authors, there is nearly 100 percent consensus on this point: passion is not a trait. People are not universally passionate about everything in their lives. Entrepreneurs are passionate about something specific. They may be passionate about multiple different objects at the same time (Cardon, et al., 2017a, 2013, 2009), or internalize their passions in different ways

(Vallerand, et al., 2003), but a critical aspect of these perspectives on passion is that it must have a focus or target. This has important implications for how passion is measured, as well as conceptualized. Of note, other authors using different definitions or conceptualizations of passion (such as how passion manifests and is displayed to other stakeholders; see Chen, et al., 2009) still agree on this particular and critical point. When studying passion, we must always consider and specify the target for which that passion is focused.

As a second important commonality, both EP and the DMP agree that the targets of entrepreneurial passion are simultaneously loved and held in high esteem. Entrepreneurial passion compels movement toward or engagement with these objects, rather than movement away from them or avoidance. In the DMP, passion is directed toward activities that people like enough that they invest time and energy in that activity (Vallerand, et al., 2003; Vallerand, 2015). In EP, passion involves positive and intense feelings that propel entrepreneurs to action (Cardon, et al., 2009).

The agreement across these conceptualizations that passion is positive and that it propels approach rather than avoidance tendencies is in contrast to some popular notions of passion stemming from certain religious traditions depicting passions that may involve suffering (e.g., the suffering of Christ). Yet, even in religious conceptualizations, it is important to remember that suffering occurs because of an overwhelming strong love of something. For example, in the case of the suffering of Christ, biblical scholars argue Christ suffered and died in an expression of God's great love for humanity. In this case, Christ's love (passion) is separable from his suffering.

While not nearly on the same scale as Christ's perseverance and sacrifice, entrepreneurs must often struggle through great challenges in order to launch, maintain, and grow their firms. Entrepreneurial passion itself involves a pleasurable phenomenological experience aimed toward a target. Pursuing that target may involve unpleasant experiences and feelings (which are separable from the actual feelings associated with passion), but the personal experience of entrepreneurial passion itself is positive. Scholars of entrepreneurial passion typically argue that when entrepreneurs feel high levels of passion for some aspect(s) of entrepreneurship, it helps motivate them to endure those struggles and persist through the challenges until they are successful (Murnieks, et al., 2016). Thus, despite the entrepreneurial journey involving both positive and negative experiences, passion is typically viewed as a positive and extremely strong phenomenon that motivates action toward the object of one's passion(s) rather than avoidance of it.

The third commonality across conceptualizations is that both EP and the DMP emphasize the important nature of one's identity relative to entrepreneurial passion. Vallerand (2015) refers to this when he discusses the person–activity interface characteristic of passion. He argues that the object about which an individual is passionate becomes internalized into the individual's identity in a way that the individual is often defined by it. For example, entrepreneurs experiencing passion would not say that they "do entrepreneurial activities," but rather that they "are entrepreneurs." The activity the entrepreneur is passionate about becomes self-defining. Similarly, the conceptualization of EP incorporates identity centrality as one of its two essential dimensions (Cardon, et al., 2009, 2013). Entrepreneurs who are passionate about inventing products would define themselves as "inventors." In this way EP is distinct from other constructs such as enthusiasm, excitement, or joy, which also involve strong positive feelings that involve approach tendencies, but for which there is not necessarily an identity connection. This identity meaning and sense of value of the object of one's passion(s) is important because it elevates the priority given to the object and also drives the individual to devote time toward engaging the passion. Both EP and the DMP agree that entrepreneurial passion is tied intricately to self-identities of the entrepreneur (see Murnieks & Cardon, 2019 for a more detailed discussion of this).

The identity component of passion is one of the key characteristics that distinguishes it from other similar constructs such as intrinsic motivation and positive emotions (e.g., Cardon, et al., 2013; Vallerand, et al., 2003; Vallerand, 2015). Whereas an individual is driven to engage in activities that are intrinsically interesting, intrinsic motivation does not presume a self-defining link between the focal activity and the person's identity. In fact, individuals may be intrinsically motivated to engage in any number of activities, from highly consequential to trivial ones. This is not the case with passions. For example, someone may be intrinsically motivated to watch a comedic film or go for a bicycle ride, yet this same individual might not identify themselves as a cinephile or as a cyclist. A similar argument can be made for distinguishing passion from positive emotions. Positive emotions can be elicited by a wide range of stimuli, many of which may have no identity-relevant component whatsoever. For example, an individual may feel joy from watching a funny movie, or elation from suddenly winning a lottery; neither of these incidents has any identity relevance though. The feelings that stem from passion also tend to be more persistent (owing to their identity connection) than those from positive affect (emotions or moods). Indeed, a recent meta-analysis confirms that passion contributes unique value to outcomes while controlling for other variables such as intrinsic motivation and job satisfaction (Pollack, et al., in press). As such, we reiterate the contention of EP and DMP scholars that passion is unique and distinct from other affective or motivational constructs.

DISTINCTIONS BETWEEN CONCEPTUALIZATIONS

While there is significant agreement about the major components of how passion is conceptualized across EP and the

DMP, there are also notable differences. Perhaps the most important one is the basic nature of the passion construct. Whereas EP characterizes entrepreneurial passion as an affective construct, the DMP explicitly defines it as a motivational one. These differences in construction have obvious implications for the basic nature of passion. According to the DMP, passion is fundamentally a motivational construct that drives individuals to engage in certain activities. The emotions and feelings experienced during this engagement occur as an outcome from the motivational drive and subsequent cognition or action. On the other hand, according to EP, entrepreneurial passion is primarily an affective construct that involves a strong, positively valenced feeling for an identity-important object. The motivation to engage in activities originates, but is separate from, this intense positive feeling.

Despite this key difference, we also note that both EP and the DMP make note of the close ties between motivation and emotions in their conceptualizations. Foundational work in the DMP notes the strong correlations between passion and positive emotions (e.g., Vallerand, et al., 2003). Similarly, the original work on EP notes the key ties between entrepreneurial passion and motivational outcomes related to goal setting, striving, and persistence in effort (e.g., Cardon, et al., 2009). In addition, the scales that are used to measure EP and the DMP include aspects of both motivation and emotion within them. For example, the DMP scale asks individuals questions about how memorable the passion experiences are or how emotionally dependent the individual is upon the activity at the core of the passion (Vallerand, et al., 2003), which probe the emotional nature of passion in the DMP. Similarly, the EP scales ask individuals about how motivated they are to make existing products better or how energized they feel from owning a company (Cardon, et al., 2013). Thus, even though each theory is specific and distinct about how it treats passion (affective vs. motivational), in practice, it is arguable that these constructs are *both* affective and motivational in nature.

A second key difference between EP and the DMP lies in their target and focus; specifically, the scales used to measure these two types of passion assess fundamentally different elements. The scales developed to assess EP measure the extent to which an individual is passionate about specific activities related to entrepreneurship. Thus, they measure *how much* passion an individual has for specific entrepreneurial activities, roles, or other objects (Cardon, et al., 2013). In contrast, the scales originally developed to assess the DMP measure the extent to which the activities are harmoniously or obsessively internalized into the individual's identity (Vallerand, et al., 2003). In practice, these scales are often used to interpret the level of harmonious or obsessive passion an individual possesses, but technically, the scales measure the type and degree of internalization; they do not measure the level or amount of passion a person experiences. This is why, in a number of studies conducted by Vallerand and his colleagues, the authors assess the level of passion toward an activity with a separate passion criteria scale (Mageau, et al., 2009; Vallerand, et al., 2003; Vallerand, et al., 2010). Surprisingly, this separate scale is not always used in studies assessing passion in general, and is typically *not* used in studies assessing passion in entrepreneurship. Importantly, we do not know whether or not the extent of entrepreneurial passion is correlated with the extent of harmonious or obsessive internalization of the target of one's passion; future research using the DMP should evaluate this possibility.

It is also important to note that both EP and the DMP stress the separation between passion and the cognitive or behavioral outcomes it drives. Both theories are explicit about the fact that entrepreneurial passion is separate and distinct from other constructs such as intrinsic motivation, commitment, persistence, zest, grit, or flow (among other things). Entrepreneurial passion studied from the perspective of both EP and the DMP may drive cognitions or behaviors related to each of these, but a clear line of demarcation exists between the entrepreneur's experience of passion and their subsequent intrinsic motivation for, commitment to, or perseverance at a task (among other outcomes). This distinguishes passion from other constructs, such as grit, which subsume a consistency of interest and zeal within the core construct (e.g., Duckworth, et al., 2007).

CONCEPTUALIZATIONS OF PASSION OTHER THAN EP AND DMP

While EP and the DMP are the most prevalent theories used to study passion to date, they are not the only ones. Here we touch on other conceptualizations of passion that have been developed. Some of these conceptualizations have focused specifically on passion in the entrepreneurial context, whereas others have examined passion more broadly in the workplace in general. In an attempt to be inclusive, we review some of the more prominent definitions of passion at work across both the entrepreneurial and other work contexts.

Baum and Locke (2004) studied entrepreneurs' passion for work, and equated passion to a love of one's work. They describe passion as encompassing love, attachment, and longing. In this case, passion is aimed at work activities in general, rather than entrepreneurship specifically, and is treated as a trait rather than as a state. This conceptualization of passion also alluded to the personal identity connection between an entrepreneur and his or her venture in saying, "passion can be witnessed ... in the tendency for entrepreneurs to experience their venture's successes and difficulties as personal events" (p. 588). This idea of identity intertwinement has been more formally acknowledged by other scholars (e.g., Cardon, et al., 2005; Shepherd & Haynie, 2009).

Chen, Yao, and Kotha (2009) define entrepreneurial passion as an intense affective state accompanied by affective, cognitive, and behavioral manifestations of high personal value. The authors further segregate these entrepreneurial passion manifestations into cognitive, affective, and behavioral dimensions, labeling the cognitive dimension as "preparedness," the affective dimension as "enthusiasm" and "passion," and the behavioral dimension as "commitment." In their study, they focused on how the manifestations of passion are perceived by others based on what the entrepreneur demonstrates (e.g., energetic body movements) rather than on what specific actions or intrapersonal outcomes passion might inspire in entrepreneurs themselves. This paper sparked an important research stream on how displayed and perceived passion impact stakeholders. Similarly, Li, Chen, Kotha, and Fisher (2017) refer to passion as an intense affective state, and also focus on how displays of passion influence others. We discuss these approaches further in Chapter 4. Here we note that there are still unanswered questions in the literature concerning how enthusiasm, preparedness, and commitment perceived by observers overlap or reconcile with EP or the DMP as experienced by entrepreneurs.

Outside of the entrepreneurship context, Jachimowicz and colleagues (2018, 2019) define passion as a strong feeling toward a personally important value/preference that sparks intentions and behaviors expressing that value/preference. This conceptualization of passion aligns with the primary elements of EP and the DMP along several key dimensions. For example, similar to EP, it defines passion as an intense affective state, it emphasizes that passion must have a target, and it asserts that this target reflects attributes with high personal value (Jachimowicz, et al., 2018, p. 9981). This approach also separates the intense affective nature from the resulting intentions and behaviors that occur as a result of passionate feelings.

One key difference between these conceptualizations of passion (e.g., Chen, et al., 2009; Jachimowicz, et al., 2019) and the more established theories of passion (e.g., EP and the DMP) is the emphasis of the latter on identity. Both EP and the DMP are explicit about the embeddedness of identity within passion. Indeed, the DMP mentions identity as a core element (Vallerand, 2015), as does EP, and EP incorporates identity-centrality questions into the scales that assess passion (Cardon, et al., 2013). Conceptualizations other than EP and the DMP typically analyze how passion is perceived by others instead of how it is experienced by the focal entrepreneur (e.g., Chen, et al., 2009; Jachimowicz, et al., 2019; Li, et al., 2017), which makes assessment of identity centrality difficult. This is perhaps why these approaches have not incorporated an identity component into their conceptualizations of passion. Based on these differences, we emphasize the importance of understanding the specific research question and what particular target(s) of passion and their identity meaning are of interest in the study based on that research question (we delve further into targets of passion in Chapter 3).

Also outside the context of entrepreneurship, Zigarmi and colleagues (2009) define work passion as a persistent, emotionally positive, meaning-based state of well-being, stemming from reoccurring cognitive and affective appraisals of various job and organizational situations that result in consistent and constructive work intentions and behaviors. Like EP and the DMP, this conceptualization treats passion as a state (not a trait). However, unlike other conceptualizations, this approach defines passion as a general state of well-being that involves cognitive and affective appraisal processes and necessitates that passion lead to both consistent and constructive intentions and behaviors. As such, this model combines the state of passion with a process model of passion including both antecedents and outcomes. Defining passion as a state of well-being invokes some complicated relationships with other constructs that would be difficult to disentangle. In contrast, in both the EP and the DMP models, antecedents and outcomes are separated from the actual construct of passion, which allows for conceptual and empirical separation and testing of passion distinct from other constructs in its nomological net. This separation allows for empirical testing of potentially functional and dysfunctional consequences of passion as well as multiple potential origins of it.

As different conceptualizations begin to emerge, we are encouraged by the efforts of numerous scholars eager to develop new insights and offer new contributions. That said, we also advocate for conceptualizations and operationalizations of passion that are precise and specific (such as those offered in the DMP and EP). We believe it is important to separate antecedents from outcomes, and to draw distinctions between passion and other similar constructs such as intrinsic motivation, enthusiasm, and excitement. Our theories of entrepreneurial passion need to set the foundation for the careful study of how and where passion originates (see Chapter 5) and how and when it creates the potential for productive and unproductive outcomes for those who experience it as well as for other stakeholders who observe displays of passion (see Chapter 4).

3. Different potential targets of entrepreneurial passion

As we discussed in Chapter 2, the two primary theories that have served as the conceptual bedrock for the study of passion in entrepreneurship are the theory of entrepreneurial passion (EP) by Cardon and her colleagues (2009, 2013) and the Dualistic Model of Passion (DMP) by Vallerand and his colleagues (2015, 2003). In both of the foundational articles for these theories (Cardon, et al., 2009; Vallerand, et al., 2003), the target for passion is set explicitly on "activities." However, since those articles were published, both sets of scholars have amended their original theories to consider a wider range of targets of passion, including but also extending beyond activities. In this chapter we discuss research that considers different objects or targets of passion, as well as the different levels of analysis of those objects (e.g., entire occupational roles such as "entrepreneur" or more specific roles such as "founder").

PASSION FOR DIFFERENT LEVELS OF TARGETS

There are different levels of abstraction at which targets of passion are viewed and conceptualized. Some studies look at passion for the overall occupation of entrepreneurship (e.g., Ho & Pollack, 2014; Murnieks, et al., 2014), primarily those based on the DMP conceptualization of passion. In contrast, most studies that invoke the theoretical lens of EP (Cardon, et al., 2009) tend to look at activities related to the particular actions of inventing products or founding and developing new companies (e.g., Breugst, et al., 2012; Cardon & Kirk, 2015). Most of these studies include all three targets of passion, but some concentrate on only one or two of those dimensions that are specific to their research question (e.g., Drnovsek, et al., 2016; Huyghe, et al., 2016).

Choosing the level of abstraction and targets of passion to include in a study is an important decision. Studying passion for entrepreneurship in general should not be equated with passion for the separate tasks involved in inventing, founding, and developing, for example. Indeed, as we discuss further in Chapter 4, research has demonstrated different effects of passion for different targets. For example, Breugst and colleagues (2012), Cardon and Kirk (2015), and Stenholm and Renko (2016) all find differential relationships between passion for different sets of activities (inventing, founding, and developing) and various constructs in the entrepreneurship process such as bricolage behaviors, persistence, and employee commitment. These studies highlight the criticality of specifying the target of passion and matching the level at which passion is studied with the particular research question under examination. Findings from one level of abstraction or pertaining to one target of passion should not be generalized to all levels or targets.

Given that passion is rooted in identities, understanding different levels of identities is helpful to understanding different levels of targets of passions. According to Brewer and Gardner (1996), individuals can hold representations of their self-concepts or self-identities at multiple levels: personal (individual), interpersonal (relational), and collective (group). This is important, because it reflects the idea that identities develop meaning for oneself in multiple ways. At the individual level, people see themselves as differentiated and possessing unique traits that define and distinguish them from others (e.g., Shepherd & Haynie, 2009). At the interpersonal level, people see themselves relating to important others through meaningful connections and role relationships. At the group level, people see themselves as parts of collectives and social groups. Indeed, Fauchart and Gruber (2011) categorized multiple founder identities using each of these different levels of analysis. From the standpoint of passion, very little work has been done to determine if these different types of identities have impacts on the type and level of passion that manifests itself. Fauchart and Gruber (2011) found very different views, motivations, and actions that result from these different types of identities. As such, we might expect significantly different manifestations of entrepreneurial passion depending on the type of identity at the center of one's passion. For instance, identities that are primarily relational or group related are likely to manifest profoundly different types of passion than those that are personal.

One way to think about objects of passion is to consider the career of an academic. We can be passionate about our occupation of academic or professor, in general, and each of us likely has a different extent to which we experience passionate feelings and/or internalize the professor identity into our self-identity, as well as the extent to which we internalize our professor passion harmoniously or obsessively. That is one level of analysis for which we could study the passion of professors. A second level would be to look at the passion we experience for sub-roles within the occupation of professor. For example, we could examine the extent or type of internalization of our passion for research, teaching, and service; our experiences of passion might vary considerably across these different sub-role targets. For instance, many professors are more passionate about their teaching and research activities than they are about their service activities and roles. A third level of analysis would be to dig deeper and consider specific aspects of each of those roles that are targets of more or less (or different internalizations of) passion. For example, within my role as a researcher (Melissa here), I identify as a theorist much more than a methodologist, and as a result my passion for developing the theoretical argumentation of papers is quite high while my passion for methodological nuance is fairly low. Similarly, entrepreneurs could have different targets of passion, which might range from a very high level of abstraction (the occupation of being an entrepreneur) to a very low level of abstraction (e.g., developing product prototypes). Studies of passion to date tend to remain within one level of abstraction only, which, as we discuss later in this chapter, might limit our complete understanding of passion and entrepreneurship.

It is notable that studies using the DMP conceptualization of harmonious and obsessive passion have primarily looked at passion for being an entrepreneur, while studies using the EP conceptualization primarily look at passion for sub-roles or sets of activities associated with entrepreneurship. The two streams do not tend to cross levels of analysis. As a result, we have no evidence concerning obsessive versus harmonious passion for inventing, founding, or developing, or with regard to how harmonious passion for one target might work with or against obsessive passion for a different target, for example. This is an opportunity for future research, which we discuss more below.

POTENTIAL TARGETS OF PASSION

Regardless of levels of analysis, authors associated with the two primary theoretical perspectives on passion in entrepreneurship have suggested a number of different specific targets for which passion can be experienced. In the case of the DMP, Vallerand (2015, p. 28) refined the definition of passion to include a range of targets covering activities, objects, other people, or even abstract concepts such as ideas or causes. Indeed, since 2003, studies analyzing passion through the lens of the DMP have expanded their scope far beyond just activities. For example, St-Louis, Carbonneau, and Vallerand (2016) and Bélanger and colleagues (2019) examined passion for different causes such as humanitarian efforts, environmentalism, and political activism. Moreover, Carbonneau, Vallerand, Lavigne, and Paquet (2016) and Ratelle, Carbonneau, Vallerand, and Mageau (2013) examined passion for specific people in romantic relationships.

In the case of EP, Cardon, Glauser, and Murnieks (2017a) reviewed extant work in prominent journals to determine what types of targets were being studied as the focus of entrepreneurial passion. The results were striking. Out of 29 papers (both conceptual and empirical) examining entrepreneurial passion, 25 (86%) were focused on some type of entrepreneurial activity. The remaining four studied some combination of objects (which was often passion for the venture itself), or the particular entrepreneurial opportunity they were pursuing. One study (Ruskin, et al., 2016) briefly looked at passion for the individual people involved in a venture. Overall, this analysis highlights the fact that passion scholars have overwhelmingly concentrated on passion for specific activities, and in the entrepreneurship context these activities are often associated with entrepreneurial roles such as inventing, founding, or developing firms (Cardon, et al., 2009). This dominant focus on activities has advanced the study of entrepreneurial passion tremendously, but it also beckons us to look wider to broaden our understanding of this construct. We need to know more about what other objects, ideas, or causes might inspire passion among entrepreneurs.

Based on the analysis discussed above, Cardon, Glauser, and Murnieks (2017a) undertook a qualitative study using interview data from 80 entrepreneurs across the United States (see Glauser, 2009). This analysis uncovered six major objects of passion among entrepreneurs (listed in order of prevalence): (1) passion for growth, (2) passion for people, (3) passion for a product or service, (4) passion for competition, (5) passion for inventing, and (6) passion for a social mission. Passion for growth indicates an affinity for building and expanding the entrepreneurial business – to scale it up and see it flourish.

This type of passion is similar to a "passion for developing" (Cardon, et al., 2009), which concentrates on activities related to nurturing, growing, and expanding a venture after it has been founded. Passion for growth is also alluded to by Cardon and colleagues (2005) when they talk about how entrepreneurs resemble parents who feel a connection to, care for, and work hard to help their children (firms). Parents (and entrepreneurs) work hard to help children (ventures) grow, and gain great satisfaction from watching them sprout and thrive. For entrepreneurs, passion for people (Cardon, et al., 2017a) indicates a strong desire to work with family, to satisfy customers, and to build meaningful relationships with employees and vendors. Interestingly, the most frequent target of this passion was not family members, but rather customers or clients. This type of entrepreneurial passion is also mentioned by Ruskin, Seymour, and Webster (2016), and reinforces the findings of other passion scholars outside entrepreneurship who find that passion for people, or for meaningful relationships with special people, can be a powerful force (e.g., Carbonneau, et al., 2016; Ratelle, et al., 2013).

Passion for products or services indicates a love for the particular object or service provided by the entrepreneurial firm. This type of passion reiterates the point made by Vallerand (2015) that passion can involve a love for certain things, such as flowers or poetry, beyond activities. In the entrepreneurial realm, a passion for a product or service is important because it highlights the fact that founders can hold an immense love for a product they sell, which is separate from a love of owning or running an entrepreneurial business itself. Many hobby entrepreneurs start businesses because they love a certain product, and feel that the product can provide joy or satisfaction to others (Warnick, 2014). This love is distinct from a passion for entrepreneurial activities or for being an entrepreneur, in general. A growing number of studies have begun to analyze the distinction between passion for a particular product or service, and a passion for the entrepreneurial venture (e.g., Clarysse, et al., 2015; Warnick, et al., 2018).

Passion for competition involves the love of being more successful than (or for beating) competitors. Cardon, Glauser, and Murnieks (2017a, p. 30) talk specifically about a love of "winning" when they discuss the passion for competition. This type of passion resembles the type of competitive fire exuded by athletes like Michael Jordan or the late Kobe Bryant. Opponents of these individuals often relate memorable, and extreme, stories of how much these athletes love to compete and, especially, to win. For example, Michael Jordan, a professional basketball player, once lost a friendly game of golf to his coach. The next day, Jordan pounded on the coach's hotel room door until he agreed to play a rematch. Jordan won, but that is less important than the fact that he simply could not let the loss from the previous day go unaddressed, even though it occurred in a sport unrelated to his expertise at basketball. Kobe Bryant, who was another professional basketball player, once dove underneath another player's legs, in a friendly practice game, during the offseason, to grab a loose ball in a meaningless contest. This play likely risked serious injury to both Kobe and the other player, but that didn't matter to Kobe as much as trying to outcompete his opponent and win. Teammates of Kobe sometimes talked about his cutthroat nature in practice games, and that even though typical one-on-one games would go on until one player reached 10 points, Kobe refused to let anyone stop until the winner had scored 100 (https://shutupnhustle.com/ 2019/08/23/kob e-bryant-work-ethic-stories/). This exemplifies a passion for competition.

Just as originally conceptualized in Cardon, Wincent, Singh, and Drnovsek (2009), Cardon, Glauser, and Murnieks (2017a) found passion for inventing to be prominent in their qualitative study of entrepreneurs. This domain of passion relates to creating new products or services, and looking for new opportunities in the market. This passion is distinct from a passion for a specific product or service because the latter focuses on the specific product or service itself whereas the former is targeted on the process of inventing and creating (e.g., tinkering with a product's design as opposed to the product itself).

Finally, passion for a social mission (Cardon, et al., 2017a) focuses on strong desires to advocate for a cause or address a need for a specific group of people. Entrepreneurs with passion for a social mission often see problems being experienced by certain individuals, or by society in general, and want to help find ways to alleviate them. Toms Shoes, Conserva Irrigation, and Pixza Pizza are all examples of companies whose founders exhibit a passion for a social mission. As we mentioned earlier in this chapter, passion for causes has been studied outside of the entrepreneurial domain by Vallerand's cohort of scholars as well.

PASSION FOR MULTIPLE TARGETS

Interestingly, the vast majority of individuals (84%) in the study by Cardon, Glauser, and Murnieks (2017a) mentioned more than one source of passion with respect to their entrepreneurial journey. This is important because it highlights the fact that individuals can, and often do, have multiple passions operating simultaneously. Cardon, Wincent, Singh, and Drnovsek (2009, p. 517) noted that "it is not necessary that entrepreneurs have a single identity that is hierarchically dominant." The implication here is that multiple salient identities could provide the basis for multiple passions. In fact, much of the research using the EP perspective includes passion for multiple targets, particularly passion for inventing, founding, and developing that was discussed in the original publication in this stream of work. We discuss outcomes associated with specific targets of passion among these three (and others) in Chapter 4.

There is less work from the DMP perspective that incorporates multiple targets of passion. This is an opportunity for further development, since recent work outside of the new venture context found interesting results when incorporating multiple targets. Schellenberg and Bailis (2015) asked undergraduate students to complete harmonious and obsessive passion measures for at least two of their favorite activities, and found that individuals with two activities about which they were harmoniously passionate reported significantly higher levels of well-being compared to those with other combinations of passion or no passion at all. These findings suggest a need for more approaches such as this that allow for multiple targets of obsessive and harmonious passion.

There has also been little research on how passions for entrepreneurial targets operate alongside passions for non-entrepreneurial targets. In a notable exception, Clarysse, Van Boxstael, and Van Hove (2015) analyzed the passion of individuals for their profession as well as for developing their businesses. They found that different targets of passion influenced venture profitability and growth through different pathways. Similarly, Huyghe, Knockaert, and Obschonka (2016, p. 345) looked at how entrepreneurial passion versus obsessive scientific passion impacted start-up intentions and spin-off intentions. Importantly, they argue that rather than individuals being driven by a singular passion, they often experience a "passion orchestra," which they define as "the intraindividual coexistence and interplay of entrepreneurial passion and passions for other non-entrepreneurial roles." These studies point out the additional variance that could be explained if we begin to broaden our analyses to include multiple passions, including passion for entrepreneurial and non-entrepreneurial targets, simultaneously.

CONSIDERATIONS WHEN STUDYING PASSION FOR MULTIPLE TARGETS

This extant work notwithstanding, there is still a gaping hole surrounding our knowledge about how multiple passions might interact to influence individual entrepreneurs. Existing work that considers multiple targets often treats them as completely independent constructs that do not interact with one another (e.g., the independent effects of harmonious and obsessive passion, or passion for inventing independently from passion for founding). Yet, there are likely numerous ways in which multiple passions might reinforce, or inhibit, one another. For example, to the extent that an individual is passionate about both people and products related to the same cause, the mechanisms behind the passions for multiple targets might combine to drive up the positive affect, identity relevance, and motivation experienced by the individual. Multiple passions might interfere with one another as well. By definition, passions require engagement and time commitment. Having multiple targets of passion could increase the time requirements felt by an individual, may introduce competing cognitive or behavioral tendencies in order to pursue each passion target, and might therefore reduce the individual's sense of autonomy in having the ability to choose to spend time engaging in other activities as well as increase conflict and stress, and reduce well-being. There may also be performance implications if multiple objects of passion cannot be pursued at the same time.

The importance of identity to the fundamental construct of passion may help advance research on how multiple targets of passion operate simultaneously for entrepreneurs. Both EP (Cardon, et al., 2009) and the DMP (Vallerand, et al., 2003) agree that identification of the activity within the individual's self-concept is a key element that distinguishes passions from other types of affect or motivation. This has important implications when we consider the variety of different types of targets that may be the focus of passion. It is easy to imagine how different targets, such as activities or people or social causes, may have different relationships with various aspects of an individual's identity. Emerging work surrounding the identities of entrepreneurs confirms the fact that they can possess multiple identities and that sometimes these identities are congruent and synergistic with one another and at other times, they are not (Powell & Baker, 2014). Congruent identities can be pursued at the same time productively, but incongruent identities, by definition, compete and conflict with one another (Powell & Baker, 2014). By extension, we would expect that feelings of passion for objects associated with incongruent identities would be problematic, while passion for objects associated with congruent identities would not be so and might even have synergistic positive effects. Future work is needed in order to examine how passions rooted in congruent or incongruent identities might have very different effects, both intrapersonally and interpersonally. For instance, cognitive dissonance and emotional labor arising from passion for incongruent identities could be extremely uncomfortable at the individual level, and might negatively impact observers at the interpersonal level.

CONSTRAINTS IMPOSED BY CURRENT MEASUREMENT SCALES AND RECOMMENDATIONS FOR FUTURE RESEARCH CONCERNING LEVELS AND TARGETS OF PASSION

The assessment of passion relative to different targets bears some discussion. First, most studies of entrepreneurial passion employ scales tied to the foundational theories discussed earlier (i.e., EP and the DMP). One side effect of using these scales is the narrowing of passion targets among subjects. More specifically, the EP and DMP scales are worded such that a target is given to the participant. For example, in the

EP scale, participants are asked how passionate they are about inventing products or founding or developing new firms. This approach constrains the entrepreneur to answering about a particular target of passion and does not allow them the freedom to answer whether or not they are more or less passionate about some other target that was not included in the questionnaire. Similarly, the use of the DMP scales in entrepreneurship typically changes the target of the scales to "being an entrepreneur" rather than allowing respondents to choose the target of their passion to use as a referent for answering questions about the extent to which that passion is harmonious or obsessive in nature. We need to be mindful of these restrictions imposed by these scales.

One approach to measuring passion employed by some DMP studies is to allow the respondent to self-report the particular activity about which they are passionate. This technique allows the respondent freedom to indicate a variety of possible targets. To date, however, this approach has only been used in DMP studies that assess passion outside of the entrepreneurial domain (e.g., Schellenberg & Bailis, 2015; Vallerand, et al., 2003). Further, empirical work to date on the effects of passion displayed by entrepreneurs on stakeholders observing that passion (e.g., Chen, et al., 2009; Mitteness, et al., 2012) also does not specify the target of the passion display that is being observed. The presumption is that if a person is demonstrating enthusiasm in a pitch to potential investors, they are passionate, yet we have no knowledge about whether they are presumed to be passionate about being an entrepreneur, their product or service, a particular set of activities associated with entrepreneurship, the opportunity to receiving funding from the potential investors, or something else entirely. This is an important opportunity for future research to discover whether the target of passion matters to observers of passionate displays.

No matter what level of analysis a researcher wants to examine for targets of passion, we implore readers to be clear and specific concerning which target(s) of passion is(are) relevant to their research question. If the question is about the extent or nature of passion for entrepreneurship, in general, that should be specified. If the research question is about the extent or nature of passion for specific sub-roles or sets of activities or other objects within the broad occupation of entrepreneur, the potential objects should be specified. And, when possible, we believe it would be fruitful for researchers to allow respondents to specify on their own what, exactly, they are passionate about that is both related to and potentially unrelated to their entrepreneurial journey, as Cardon, Glauser, and Murnieks (2017a) did. This would help us to better understand the different targets of passion that exist for entrepreneurs and how the interplay of various targets and the extent of passions and types of internalization of those passions (harmonious and obsessive) operate together in terms of how they originate (see Chapter 5) and the impacts they generate for entrepreneurs, their firms, and other stakeholders (see Chapter 4).

4. The profits and perils that can arise from entrepreneurial passion

Now that we have discussed different conceptualizations of what entrepreneurial passion is in Chapter 2, and what entrepreneurial passion might be felt for (different targets) in Chapter 3, we turn our attention to why we should care about studying passion in the first place. What does passion do to or for entrepreneurs? We organize this discussion along two dimensions. First, we review evidence concerning how experienced passion impacts an entrepreneur's thoughts, emotions, behaviors, and firm outcomes. Second, we examine the outcomes that tend to arise when an entrepreneur showcases or displays their passion to other key stakeholders such as potential investors (crowdfunders, angel investors, venture capitalists, etc.) and current or potential employees. In discussing these relationships, our intention is not to offer a comprehensive review of all known studies involving entrepreneurial passion. Rather, our focus lies on providing a selective, but representative, overview of the key findings to date, and their implications. For those interested in more comprehensive coverage, we refer you to recent literature reviews by Newman, Obschonka, Moeller, and Chandan (2019) and Schwarte, Song, and Hunt (2019), and meta-analyses on passion by Curran and colleagues (2015) and Pollack, Ho, O'Boyle, and Kirkman (in press).

Before diving into the details about the effects of entrepreneurial passion, it is essential that we note that (1) not all entrepreneurs need to be passionate to be successful, and (2) passion alone will not lead to success. While some individuals are pulled into entrepreneurship out of love for a product or service, social cause, or desire to be an entrepreneur, and therefore may be more likely to develop passion (see Chapter 5 for further discussion of this), others are pushed into entrepreneurship out of necessity due to lack of other job opportunities. Still other entrepreneurs may have a keen ability to see a profitable opportunity and the resources to act on that opportunity that takes them on to large financial success. While each of these different types of entrepreneurs may develop entrepreneurial passion, they may not. More importantly, they need not in order to be successful. Based on all of the research to date on passion and entrepreneurship (discussed further below), we suggest that passion is a value-added element that increases engagement and motivation, helps individuals persevere and move forward despite challenges, negative feedback, or market downturns, and helps individuals enjoy their entrepreneurial pursuit in meaningful ways. However, passion is not a magical elixir that single-handedly makes an entrepreneur successful. Within the field, we do not have any empirical evidence that entrepreneurial passion is either a necessary or a sufficient condition to guarantee success. Indeed, strong research designs that control for known, important success factors such as idea quality, market potential, and the particular skill set of the entrepreneur, and then evaluate the unique added influence of passion (e.g., Mitteness, et al., 2012), are rare. More work using robust designs like these are needed (see Chapter 7 for more discussion on future research).

In the sections that follow, we review the extant work on entrepreneurial passion, with a particular emphasis on the positive and negative effects that emanate from (1) the experience of passion by entrepreneurs (intraindividual), and (2) the display of passion to stakeholders (interindividual).

POSITIVE IMPACTS (POTENTIAL PROFITS) OF EXPERIENCED PASSION

Entrepreneurial passion is primarily a positive force for the individuals that experience it and for their organizations, and there is a large variety of work that examines the influences of passion on different outcomes such as individual cognitions and behaviors, and firm performance and growth. We focus first on individual outcomes such as cognitions, emotions, and behaviors before discussing firm outcomes below.

Because passion involves intense feelings for important identities (discussed in Chapter 2), and individuals are driven to verify important identities (McCall & Simmons, 1966; Murnieks, et al., 2014), passion typically leads individuals to think and act in ways that reinforce or bolster the identities that ground their passions. Individuals are also motivated to maintain positive feelings they experience, and therefore work hard to ensure reinforcement of the positive feelings and motivational components of passion.

The main cognition that has been associated with passion is entrepreneurial self-efficacy (ESE). ESE is a person's perception of their own capabilities to achieve specific outcomes (Audia, et al., 2000; Bandura, 1991), and in this case, an entrepreneur's belief in their abilities to perform tasks related to their role as an entrepreneur such as developing new ideas, establishing a position in product markets, or making decisions under conditions of risk and uncertainty (Chen, et al., 1998; Forbes, 2005). Passion is associated with ESE because individuals often derive enjoyment from engaging in activities where they have a strong belief in their ability to succeed (Baum & Locke, 2004; Cardon & Kirk, 2015). Also, because people engage more in activities they enjoy, they are likely to develop greater skill and competence through repeated engagement, which then increases their ESE for that activity even more. Indeed, empirical work surrounding entrepreneurial passion finds support for both these relationships: ESE leads to entrepreneurial passion (Cardon & Kirk, 2015), and vice versa (Murnieks, et al., 2014). Looking at this holistically then, ESE and entrepreneurial passion likely work in a reciprocating, reinforcing loop.

Perhaps more importantly, passion and ESE are both strong drivers of psychological and behavioral outcomes such as entrepreneurial persistence, grit, and resilience. Persistence involves "continuation of effortful action despite failures, impediments, or threats, either real or imagined" (Gimeno, et al., 1997, p. 758). It is similar to tenacity, which involves sustained action and energy despite obstacles (Baum & Locke, 2004), and grit, which has been defined as "an individual's perseverance toward long-term goals" (Mueller, et al., 2017, p. 260). Such factors are critical in entrepreneurship because founding, maintaining, and growing a firm involve numerous obstacles and high failure rates (Markman, et al., 2005; Wennberg, et al., 2010). Entrepreneurs have to persist through such obstacles in order to be successful. Persistent behavior involves goal-directed energy and sustained activity over time (Seo, et al., 2004; Seo, et al., 2010), and often requires multiple attempts and repeated efforts in the face of adversity and challenges (Markman, et al., 2005; Wu, et al., 2007). Research evidence is strong that passion drives individuals to persist in their entrepreneurial efforts, regardless of any setbacks or challenges they face (Cardon & Kirk, 2015). Harmonious passion for entrepreneurship, in particular, leads to entrepreneurs spending more time working on their ventures (Murnieks, et al., 2014), and passion for inventing and passion for founding have strong effects on entrepreneurs persisting through setbacks (Cardon & Kirk, 2015).

Besides persistence, entrepreneurial passion also has the ability to drive other important aspects of the entrepreneurial process such as goal pursuit, including setting more challenging goals, being more committed to goals once set, and sustained striving toward achieving those goals (Cardon, et al., 2009; Drnovsek, et al., 2016; Fisher, et al., 2018). In entrepreneurship, goals are powerful motivators of behavior because they direct attention, action, intensity, and duration of effort toward desired outcomes (Drnovsek, et al., 2016; Kuratko, et al., 1997; Locke & Latham, 1990). When individuals are passionate about a target, they are more likely to be committed to and tenacious toward achieving goals associated with that target (Cardon, et al., 2009; Drnovsek, et al., 2016; Fisher, et al., 2018). These findings reinforce our discussion in Chapter 2 of how passion inspires action and forward motion for those who feel it.

Passion has also been associated with pre-emergent venture cognitions and behaviors such as creativity and entrepreneurial alertness (Campos, 2017), scanning and search behaviors (Turner & Gianiodis, 2018), opportunity recognition (Bao, et al., 2017), and the employment of effectual versus causal logics in venture pursuit (Stroe, et al., 2018). More specifically, harmonious passion (although not sufficient by itself) is central to the use of effectuation (e.g., Sarasvathy, 2001), while obsessive passion is instead associated with the use of causation (Stroe, et al., 2018). For individuals pursuing innovations within university contexts, higher levels of passion for entrepreneurship are associated with greater spin-off and start-up intentions (Huyghe, et al., 2016).

Even after venture founding, passion still has strong effects on entrepreneurial behavior, which can then affect venture outcomes. For example, entrepreneurs with higher passion for inventing and developing are more likely to engage in bricolage behaviors (being resourceful through creative manipulation of available assets), which elevates chances for venture survival (Stenholm & Renko, 2016). Moreover, Ho and Pollack (2014) find that harmoniously passionate entrepreneurs are more likely to discuss business issues with other people (increasing their out-degree network centrality) than obsessively passionate entrepreneurs (who have lower in-degree network centrality). As a result, harmonious entrepreneurial passion leads to higher levels of business income from peer referrals whereas obsessive entrepreneurial passion decreases business income from referrals (Ho & Pollack, 2014). Entrepreneurial passion also shows powerful ties to goal-related cognitions and behaviors that can influence firm performance. For example, entrepreneurial passion for developing ventures leads to greater goal commitment, which increases venture growth (Drnovsek, et al., 2016). Entrepreneurial passion for developing also demonstrates significant relationships to the goal-pursuit self-regulation modes of locomotion and self-assessment (Mueller, et al., 2017). Whereas locomotion tends to promote higher grit and firm performance, self-assessment has the opposite effect (Mueller, et al., 2017). This last study shows that entrepreneurial passion for developing has important effects on firm performance, but importantly, that these effects are mediated by self-regulation (locomotion and assessment) and grit.

As this section indicates, the experience of entrepreneurial passion can lead to strong and typically positive effects on cognitions and behaviors. Empirical evidence links entrepreneurial passion to entrepreneurial self-efficacy (Cardon & Kirk, 2015; Murnieks, et al., 2014), creativity (Cardon, et al., 2013), entrepreneurial intentions (Huyghe, et al., 2016), goal commitment (Drnovsek, et al., 2016), persistence (Cardon & Kirk, 2015; Murnieks, et al., 2016), goal pursuit (Drnovsek, et al., 2016), and ultimately, better firm performance (Drnovsek, et al., 2016; Ho & Pollack, 2014; Mueller, et al., 2017; Stenholm & Renko, 2016).

NEGATIVE EFFECTS (POTENTIAL PERILS) OF EXPERIENCED PASSION

While entrepreneurial passion definitely possesses the ability to drive positive outcomes, empirical evidence also demonstrates that there are potential downsides to entrepreneurial passion, especially when that passion is obsessive. Obsessive entrepreneurial passion represents a state where the individual feels compelled to engage in the target activity, and often does so in a manner that conflicts with other activities or life domains. Empirical evidence indicates that obsessive entrepreneurial passion is positively related to burnout (de Mol, et al., 2018), role conflict, and role overload (Thorgren & Wincent, 2013), while harmonious entrepreneurial passion shows the opposite effect. In turn, role conflict has a negative effect on opportunity search, which suggests that harmonious entrepreneurial passion helps, while obsessive passion hinders, such search (Thorgren & Wincent, 2013).

As noted above, because passion involves strong feelings and motivations that are tied to important identities, it can lead to perseverance through adversities (Cardon, et al., 2009; Cardon & Kirk, 2015; Mueller, et al., 2017). The other side of the passion coin is that it can also lead to rigidity in direction and a failure to pivot business ideas based on important feedback from customers or investors (Ho & Pollack, 2014; Mitteness, et al., 2012). Unfortunately, passion can also make it very hard for entrepreneurs to recognize when their ventures are failing and to shut them down (and conserve resources), leading to destructive persistence (Shepherd, et al., 2009). Passion can even push entrepreneurs to hold on to their firms and avoid selling them even when they are quite successful due to the deep identity intertwinement between entrepreneurs and their ventures (Cardon, et al., 2005; Shepherd & Haynie, 2009).

Ultimately, when unchecked, passion can be harmful. Empirical evidence on this, although limited, suggests that obsessive entrepreneurial passion, in particular, lowers venture performance (Adomdza & Baron, 2013; Ho & Pollack, 2014). That said, we are unaware of any studies that find negative performance implications of harmonious entrepreneurial passion, or of entrepreneurial passion for inventing, founding, or developing. Obviously, this is an area in need of deeper empirical investigation.

UNKNOWN EFFECTS OF EXPERIENCED PASSION

In their original conceptual work, Cardon, Wincent, Singh, and Drnovsek (2009, p. 527) suggested that "what passion does varies, depending on (1) what the passion is for (e.g., which identity is involved and how salient that is to the individual), (2) which specific entrepreneurial behavior is considered, (3) which particular goal cognitions [or other mediators] are activated, and (4) what aspect of entrepreneurial effectiveness is of substantive interest." Over a decade later, we concur with their arguments that there are "parallel and dynamic pathways for passion's effects, rather than simple linear relationships." To that end, a lot of work remains to be done in order to fill in the gaps in our knowledge concerning the potential effects of passion in entrepreneurship.

The outcomes of interest and relationships between entrepreneurial passion and those outcomes depend in large part on the specific conceptualization of passion, and literature remains fragmented concerning how different conceptualizations of passion may impact the same outcomes. For example, while different targets of entrepreneurial passion (EP) are often included in the same models in order to determine their differential and incremental effects (e.g., passions for inventing and developing are associated with persistence while passion for growth is not; Cardon & Kirk, 2015), and harmonious passion (HP) and obsessive passion (OP) are also included in comparative analyses (e.g., Ho & Pollack, 2014), studies that incorporate both EP and HP/OP are quite rare. There are only two studies we could find that incorporated both conceptualizations and empirical measures of passion of entrepreneurs. The first was a scale development paper designed to demonstrate that EP is distinct from HP and OP (Cardon, et al., 2013), and was specifically not designed to examine the relative explanatory power of the different conceptualizations of passion on outcomes of interest. The second by Huyghe, Knockaert, and Obschonka (2016) compared the relative impact of entrepreneurial passion for inventing using the EP conceptualization and obsessive passion for scientific research activities using the Dualistic Model of Passion (DMP) conceptualization. This paper makes important strides in incorporating both conceptualizations, but still does not allow for full comparison of EP and HP/OP for the same targets. Thus, we do not know how different manners of passion internalization for different targets (e.g., HP for inventing vs. OP for inventing) might differentially influence outcomes such as goal striving, persistence, ESE, or entrepreneurial intentions, much less firm performance or growth. This is a major oversight in the literature on passion in entrepreneurship to date, and one we strongly encourage scholars to rectify going forward.

We also have limited knowledge concerning what happens when the strong positive force of passion collides with powerful negative forces such as grief associated with failure (e.g., Shepherd, 2003). Recent work finds that although fear of failure leads to higher negative emotions from challenging events, HP dampens this negative effect, while OP magnifies it (Stroe, et al., in press). This suggests powerful interactions between negative emotions associated with failure (fear, grief) and positive emotions of passion, with potentially mixed outcomes depending on the specific object or type of passion involved. We need more empirical work that examines how different forms or targets of passion co-exist with other characteristics of entrepreneurs such as fear of failure, as well as how cognitive, behavioral, and performance reactions and outcomes to daily positive and negative emotional events influence and are influenced by those characteristics. For example, do feelings of passion make entrepreneurs respond more dramatically to positive and negative affective events that occur, such as securing a big sale or losing a key customer? Or do feelings of passion and the strength and stability of the identities they are based on instead help regulate the daily emotional roller-coaster entrepreneurs typically experience such that potential profits are maximized while potential perils are minimized? See Chapter 7 for more discussion of opportunities for future research on the experience of passion of entrepreneurs.

IMPACTS OF DISPLAYED AND PERCEIVED PASSION ON OTHER STAKEHOLDERS

Throughout this book, we attempt to be clear about the distinctions between experienced and displayed/perceived entrepreneurial passion. These are not the same thing, and we need to be careful about interpreting or generalizing results from findings about each specific form of passion (experienced, displayed, and perceived) to the other forms of passion. This shift in focus from the person experiencing passion to other stakeholders that may perceive how passionate the entrepreneur is based on their passionate displays is important. Yet, the scales used to measure displayed and perceived passion are distinct from those that measure experienced passion, primarily because the former do not capture the identity meaningfulness of the passion target as the latter do. Therefore, it is essential that we recognize that we are no longer talking about the experience of passion for entrepreneurs, but rather how they display that passion to other people, and perhaps more importantly, the extent to which other stakeholders perceive the entrepreneur to be passionate (Cardon, et al., 2017b; Chen, et al., 2009; Mitteness, et al., 2012). In the sections that follow, we review a representative sample of studies that assess displayed and perceived passion and examine the effects that have been discovered.

THE PROFITS AND PERILS OF DISPLAYED AND PERCEIVED PASSION ON POTENTIAL INVESTORS

One of the most powerful things about entrepreneurial passion is the fact that it has the ability to infuse and inspire more than the focal entrepreneur; it is contagious (Cardon, 2008). In fact, venture investors often talk about the fact that one primary reason they search for passionate entrepreneurs is for the contagion effect (e.g., Murnieks, et al., 2016). Investors know that the fire of entrepreneurial passion can spread rapidly in a new firm, and galvanize and motivate an entire team. It is perhaps not surprising then that a number of studies have looked at the effects of entrepreneurial passion in the new venture investing context. The majority of work on displays of passion has focused on external stakeholders of potential investors, including angel investors, venture capitalists (VCs), and crowdfunders. This is important because although different types of investors are fairly distinct in the specific criteria they use in making investment decisions, as well as in the magnitude of investments they make and their level of individual decision-making control about making such investments, the findings concerning the importance of passion to investor decision-making are fairly robust across investor types.

Harkening back to our previous discussion about how displayed passion is assessed in these studies, we categorize this work into different groups. One group uses quasi-experimental designs like conjoint thought experiments that provide the investor with hypothetical investment scenarios (e.g., Hsu, et al., 2017; Shepherd & Zacharakis, 1999). In these scenarios, investors are told that the entrepreneurs being evaluated have varying levels of entrepreneurial passion (along with other qualities), and the conjoint experiment then assesses what effect these various levels of passion and other qualities have on investment choices such as likelihood of investing funds. In these designs, investors implicitly assume that their perception of the qualities of the entrepreneur, such as passion (whether it is high or low), are accurate. Among these studies, displayed entrepreneurial passion is clearly linked to higher probabilities of investment (e.g., Murnieks, et al., 2016; Warnick, et al., 2018). For example, Murnieks and colleagues (2016) found that angel investors value passion in addition to tenacity, as well as both together, and that greater entrepreneurial experience of the investors magnified those effects. As another example, Warnick, Murnieks, McMullen, and Brooks (2018) confirmed that investors were positively influenced by displayed entrepreneurial passion, as well as by displays of passion for their products. Interestingly, Warnick and colleagues (2018) also found that these effects were enhanced for entrepreneurs who showed openness to receiving feedback from investors on their ideas.

A second group of studies in this research space looks at actual displays of passion by entrepreneurs, and assesses their effects on investor evaluations. These studies typically have the investors themselves rate how much passion they perceive during the entrepreneur's presentation (e.g., Mitteness, et al., 2012) or the extent to which they believe the entrepreneur exhibited enthusiastic displays of their latent passion (Cardon, et al., 2017b). In one of the first studies conducted on the effect of displayed entrepreneurial passion, Chen, Yao, and Kotha (2009) proposed that when entrepreneurs experience passion, it is likely accompanied by manifestations of passion that include enthusiasm (observable demonstrations of very positive emotions for their venture, product, or service), preparedness (the extent to which the entrepreneur has thought about and thought through specific aspects of their business), and commitment (behavioral demonstrations of the extent of determination an individual has to attain a goal; Hollenbeck & Klein, 1987). Each of these factors might impact stakeholders in terms of how much they want to and do support the entrepreneur who displays that manifestation or outcome. Using data from a business plan competition with a variety of different types of investors involved, Chen and colleagues' (2009) original findings indicated that preparedness, not displayed passion (measured as enthusiasm), impacts investors' decisions to fund ventures.

This paper sparked a stream of work that has attempted to tease apart these effects with specific types of investors such as angels, VCs, and crowdfunders. For example, Mitteness, Sudek, and Cardon (2012) found that investor ratings of how passionate they perceived an entrepreneur to be positively influenced their evaluations of funding potential. Interestingly, the strength of this effect varied substantially depending on a number of specific characteristics of the angels themselves (e.g., age, cognitive style, openness to experience, promotion versus prevention focus, etc.). Similarly, Li, Chen, Kotha, and Fisher (2017) found that enthusiasm displayed in the introductory videos of a crowdfunding project was contagious and increased viewers' enthusiasm, financial contributions, and campaign sharing to others. Further, higher perceived project innovativeness strengthened the positive effect of displayed enthusiasm on social-media exposure and funding for the project (Li, et al., 2017). Displayed passion can also operate as a mediating factor influencing potential investors. For example, Oo, Allison, Sahaym & Juasrikul (2019) found that perceived passion mediated the influence of user entrepreneurship on crowdfunding success or failure.

The majority of empirical evidence in this space finds that displays of enthusiasm along with other factors are more likely to influence investor evaluations than enthusiasm alone. For example, investor perceptions of the passion of the entrepreneur along with creativity of their product have been found to jointly influence funding success, and this effect may occur through a contagion process where the potential investors have an affective reaction to the passionate displays (Davis, et al., 2017). Displays of passion may also influence funding potential through status conferral, but only if observers believe the passion expression is appropriate and agree with the target of that expression (Jachimowicz, et al., 2019). Importantly, potential investors may not commit funds to entrepreneurs they perceive as inauthentic, and we need more work on the nature, prevalence, and effects of inauthenticity of entrepreneurs as it pertains to potential investors (Martens, et al., 2007).

In a direct test of all three of Chen and colleagues' (2009) proposed manifestations of passion, Cardon, Mitteness, and Sudek (2017b) found that the extent to which preparedness matters to angel investors depends on the extent to which entrepreneurs invested their own money in the venture (their commitment). When entrepreneurs invested a lot of personal money in their ventures, preparedness has a positive effect on funding potential, but when that personal investment was low, preparedness has no effect on funding potential. Similarly, enthusiastic displays of passion can be important to angel investors, but that importance depends on the way in which entrepreneurs demonstrate commitment (e.g., how much of their own money they invested, how much time they spent pursuing their ventures, or the extent to which they used money efficiently prior to their pitch). Not surprisingly, enthu-siasm has a negative impact on funding potential when entre-preneurs had already invested a lot of time and money in their ventures without using it efficiently or making substantial progress, yet when those signals are not present, enthusiastic displays have a positive impact on angel evaluations (Cardon, et al., 2017b).

Although the studies discussed above utilize different conceptualizations and measurement of displays or manifes-tations of passion, the consistent theme across them is that enthusiasm alone is not enough to secure investor interest or funding. Instead, investors are only likely to take the entrepre-neur seriously if the enthusiastic display is accompanied by preparedness or commitment (Cardon, et al., 2017b) or other factors (e.g., openness to feedback; Warnick, et al., 2018) that indicate the entrepreneur has qualities other than just being enthusiastic about their product, service, firm, or potential as an entrepreneur. Perhaps more importantly, we agree that "the relationships between experienced passion, enthusiasm, preparedness, and commitment are open to conceptual and empirical examination ... but should not be subsumed under the broad term of 'passion'" (Cardon, et al., 2017b, p. 1076).

CAUTIONS ABOUT CONSTRUCT CLARITY AND MEASUREMENT CONCERNING DISPLAYED/PERCEIVED PASSION

The process of rating passion displays used in most of this research bears more discussion. Some scales used to assess displays of entrepreneurial passion ask individuals to rate the degree of animated expressions and energetic movements the entrepreneur displays. Of note, identity centrality is often not assessed in these scales. As we stressed in Chapter 2, one of the key elements that separates all types of passion from other constructs such as intrinsic motivation and positive affect is the tie to identity. Thus, scales that do not assess identity risk conflating entrepreneurial passion with enthusiasm, energy, or displayed motivation. There is undoubtedly some correlation between these constructs and entrepreneurial passion, but we need to be careful about equating them, or from drawing conclusions about displayed passion when the assessed measure may have captured something different, such as enthusiasm, good presentation skills, or salesmanship.

Importantly, Cardon, Mitteness, and Sudek (2017b) argue that while enthusiasm might be aligned with outward displays of passion, both preparedness and commitment are potential outcomes of passion experienced by an entrepreneur that could also be present regardless of the entrepreneur's passion. Said differently, an entrepreneur can and should be prepared to pitch their venture; they should have thought through the business idea quite thoroughly, whether or not they feel a strong emotional, motivation, and identity connection to that firm (aka, passion). Entrepreneurs should also be committed to their ventures through demonstrating their strong desire to achieve their goals, often through personal investment, which does not require passion for their venture, product, or any entrepreneurial role to be felt. As such, enthusiasm, preparedness, and commitment may be associated with experiences of passion for entrepreneurs, but are not necessarily so, and therefore are distinct constructs. This is why we encourage the use of more precise terms such as "displayed passion" or "enthusiasm" rather than the more general term of "passion" for this work.

UNKNOWN EFFECTS OF DISPLAYED/ PERCEIVED ENTREPRENEURIAL PASSION ON POTENTIAL INVESTORS

Quite shockingly, we do not have direct evidence that analyzes the true correlation between experienced passion, displayed passion, and perceived passion. Namely, we do not know enough about how the experience of passion by the entrepreneur aligns with their display of passion to others (such as through animated gestures or facial expressions). Moreover, we need more investigation about the degree to which this alignment is accurately perceived by external observers (who then may or may not believe those gestures and expressions truly indicate the person feels entrepreneurial passion). Instead, the vast majority of extant research rests on the implicit assumptions put forth by Chen and colleagues (2009) that when an entrepreneur feels passion it will most likely manifest in their animated gestures (their apparent enthusiasm or excitement), their preparedness (ability to talk competently about their business idea), and their commitment to their ventures (extent to which they have invested personal resources such as time and money into the venture), which will all be important to other stakeholders. As a body of researchers we have somehow presumed that such displays of enthusiasm, preparedness, and/or commitment are evidence that the person displaying them is passionate. However, we have yet to verify whether this may or may not be an accurate presumption.

In surveying the literature, we have noticed a wide variety of interpretations of displayed passion. A number of opera-tionalizations of displayed or perceived "passion" are actually assessing enthusiasm, or demonstrations of excitement, joy, and positive energy. Therefore, we believe a dose of caution is warranted lest we allow entrepreneurial passion to be con-fused with these other constructs. The foundational theories of entrepreneurial passion have taken great care to establish it as a unique element that is distinguishable and separate from other psychological constructs. As such, we do NOT advocate for displays of animated facial/vocal expressions or expressive body language to be labeled passion, but instead suggest it would be more accurately called "enthusiasm," as Chen and colleagues (2009) originally label it. Indeed, empir-ical evidence suggests that studying the specific elements of enthusiasm, preparedness, and commitment yields much more detailed and nuanced relationships for how they impact potential investors than more common approaches that treat enthusiastic displays as "passion" (e.g., Cardon, et al., 2017b).

THE PROFITS AND PERILS OF DISPLAYED AND PERCEIVED PASSION ON EMPLOYEES

Much less focus has been given to how displays of passion by entrepreneurs influence non-investor stakeholders such as current or potential employees. This is interesting given that over ten years ago, Cardon (2008) suggested that passion may be contagious to a variety of entrepreneurial stakeholders, and encouraged work on how passion of entrepreneurs, along with other factors, might influence employees and potential employees. One empirical study (Breugst, et al., 2012) of such effects found that the passion of entrepreneurs can indeed be contagious to employees, as it generates positive affect, which subsequently influences their affective commitment. Interestingly, these effects depend on the particular target of the entrepreneur's passion. More specifically, employee perceptions of their supervisor's entrepreneurial passion for inventing and developing enhance employees' commitment to their ventures, but perceptions of passion for founding reduce it. These effects are partially mediated by the employees' experiences of positive affect at work, as well as clarity in the goals the entrepreneur communicates.

Also quite interestingly, the Breugst, Domurath, Patzelt, and Klaukien (2012) empirical study is the only one we are aware of that has developed and implemented scales for stakeholders to evaluate their perceptions of an entrepreneur's passion for specific targets, here inventing, founding, and developing. Although these observer evaluations are positively and significantly correlated across targets, the correlations are moderate (.37 to .48), suggesting that observers can discern differential levels of passion an entrepreneur displays for different targets. This suggests that other research on how passionate displays influence stakeholders could also examine this at a more nuanced level by differentiating among passionate displays for different objects/targets. We suspect that, as Breugst and colleagues (2012) found, just as we know that different targets of experienced passion have differential effects on cognitive, behavioral, and performance outcomes for entrepreneurs and their firms, so should different targets of passion have differential effects on the cognitive, behavioral, and decisional outcomes of observers perceiving that passion. It seems important to determine if the effects of displayed or perceived passion on potential investors or potential employees differ based on the target of that passion or its internalization. Do potential investors care what an entrepreneur is passionate about? Do they care whether that passion is experienced harmoniously or obsessively? Can they tell? We do not yet have answers to those questions.

Here we suggest that we need a lot more research on how passion influences other stakeholders of firms, such as potential partners, potential employees, or friends and family that might provide household or social support for the entrepreneur and the firm. We encourage anyone conducting that work to examine not just displays or perceptions of passion at a general level, but also to incorporate different targets of passion in order to determine if perceptions of an entrepreneur's passion for different targets or passion internalized in different ways have differential effects for observers as they do for entrepreneurs who experience that passion.

5. Stoking the fires of entrepreneurial passion through engagement, education, and contagion

Given the myriad of positive outcomes that arise from both experiencing and displaying passion to others, the obvious questions concern how to spark the initial fire of passion and stoke that fire to the point where it has the beneficial effects discussed in Chapter 4, and how to contain the fire so that it does not burn out of control and create the detrimental effects also discussed in the previous chapter. Unfortunately, there is no magic pill, no book, and no quick test that allows you to "discover your passion," "find your passion," or "ignite the fire that fuels your life's work," which are all common sayings in the popular literature. Ironically, finding one's passion is rarely something that occurs instantaneously. Passions are not treasures that lie hidden beneath the surface of a person's self-concept, just waiting to be unearthed. On the contrary, entrepreneurial passions need to be nurtured and developed, much like children (Cardon, et al., 2005). Discovering one's passions often involves learning over time, trial and error, and deliberate and concerted effort.

Interestingly, there is quite a dearth of academic research on how passion might be found or developed, and thus it is a topic in desperate need of future research. What we do know is that developing passion requires choosing to spend time engaging with the target of the passion as well as valuing or preferring that target above others (Vallerand, 2015). Both of these conditions are necessary precursors to internalizing the target as part of one's identity, which is a core component of passion. Current research suggests that there are three primary paths to the development of passion: (1) engaging in work for which one ultimately develops a passion, (2) learning more about what it means to be an entrepreneur through formal or informal education, which also involves engaging in entrepreneurial work, and (3) interacting with passionate others who infect the focal person through contagion processes. We discuss each in turn.

DEVELOPING PASSION THROUGH ENGAGING IN ACTIVITIES

The Ewing Marion Kauffman Foundation claims that over 10 percent of US startups are founded by individuals who never intended to start firms (Robb & Reedy, 2012). Called different names such as "user entrepreneurs," "accidental entrepreneurs," or "hobby entrepreneurs," these individuals are defined by the fact that they formed their firms either by (1) taking something they already loved doing and monetizing it, or (2) by creating a product to meet a particular need they had for which there was no existing product or market. Evidence of the second group is provided by Fauchart and Gruber (2011, p. 947), who note that a large number of founders (whom they label communitarians) are motivated by the creation of "a product for their own use because their own customer needs are not satisfied by current market offerings." Prominent examples of this are Sara Blakely of Spanx, Nick Woodman of GoPro, and Drew Houston of Dropbox.

Most commonly called hobby or user entrepreneurs, the first group develops passion by focusing intently on crafting their particular product or service. This often leads to a desire to share that passion, as well as the product, with their broader community. For example, in 2001 Brian Frankle was in search of a durable yet ultralight backpack for his 2,600 mile end-to-end thru-hike of the Pacific Crest Trail. Not finding what he wanted, he made his own pack. Other hikers saw it and wanted to know where they could get one. What started as a small firm in Brian's garage, Ultralight Adventure Equipment (ULA), is now a thriving and growing firm that supplies a large variety of backpacks to hikers of all kinds. Similarly, Feathered Friends is a firm founded by Peter and Carol Hickner to make the outdoor gear they wanted to use but could not find or afford (https://featheredfriends.com/pages/about-us). Founded in 1972, today this company is run by a second generation of the family and regularly wins awards for innovative, durable, and responsibly sourced products.

The joy these entrepreneurs experienced from doing some activity such as backpacking or traveling played an important role in helping to spark their passion. Over time, continued engagement with an activity and the repeated experiences of joy and elation help to instantiate an activity into one's identity, which leads to development of passion. Prior work has noted that user entrepreneurs tend to experience enjoyment and show that to others as they create innovative products inspired by their personal experiences (Oo, et al., 2019; Stock, et al., 2015). Of note, the joy and self-identification with the activity or product (both components of passion) can occur before the individual decides to turn that into a business venture, because individuals can find meaning and personal fulfillment in the role identity associated with their hobby or product (Burke, 2006; Stryker & Burke, 2000). They can be passionate for their hobby or a product they have created, regardless of whether or not they become entrepreneurs. Yet, passion developed from leisure or hobby activities is one of the key drivers for hobby or user entrepreneurs to found their firms (Guercini & Ranfagni, 2016; Hamdi-Kidar & Vellera, 2018). As we mentioned in Chapter 2, both intensely positive feelings and an identity connection to the target of those feelings are critical components of passion. Importantly, the target of passion can include more than just engaging in certain types of activities (e.g., backpacking). For example, social entrepreneurs are often driven by a pro-social identity based on a desire to help certain populations (e.g., refugees, animals, natural ecosystems) or address certain social needs (e.g., having clean drinking water, preserving the environment) prior to creating a social venture (Conger, et al., 2018). Passion for social change can lead entrepreneurs to engage in activities that create and share value with others (Hlady Rispal & Servantie, 2017).

These examples and research suggest that entrepreneurial passion can arise even though an individual's initial passion was non-entrepreneurial in nature. Engagement with certain activities, causes, or populations can drive a realization of both an inherent interest and identity importance with the target, as well as positive and intense feelings, both of which are critical components of the development of passion. Individuals who create a product for their own personal use and enjoy that use so much often want to share it with others. Or, sometimes others see a new product and insist on being able to use that product for their own purpose. In this way, hobby or user entrepreneurs can end up with an accidental business that blossoms, often fueled by their passion for the product or the population they are serving as much as for the company or for being an entrepreneur.

Alternatively, people may start a business due to hopes of financial gains, and once they have devoted considerable time and effort into that business, come to develop a passion for it. This may be due to resolving cognitive dissonance ("I spend so much time doing this, I must love it!") or simply growing affection for the activity one spends considerable time doing. The original conceptualization of entrepreneurial passion by Cardon, Wincent, Singh, and Drnovsek explicitly argued that passion "is aroused not because some entrepreneurs are inherently disposed to such feelings but, rather, because they are engaged in something that relates to a meaningful and salient self-identity for them" (2009, p. 516). Indeed, recent empirical research confirms the importance that spending time engaging in an activity has for the development of feelings that are part of passion (Gielnik, et al., 2015; Mageau, et al., 2009).

Across two studies, Gielnik and colleagues (2015) found that individuals who expend effort toward entrepreneurial activities develop greater feelings of passion the following week, and that making progress and having free choice to engage in those activities helps explain that relationship. Even though the authors did not measure the identity centrality of these passionate feelings, their findings are relevant here because while we know that becoming an entrepreneur takes considerable effort, so does maintaining progress and continuing to pursue an entrepreneurial career. Typically, this process is not steady or smooth, and there are repeated cycles of both successes and setbacks (Collewaert, et al., 2016; Gielnik, et al., 2015; Lichtenstein, et al., 2007). As such, not just entrepreneurial activity engagement, but also making progress through that activity engagement, seems to be an important aspect of the development of feelings of passion (Gielnik, et al., 2015). Indeed, comprehensive longitudinal work on the dynamic nature of entrepreneurial passion suggests that although the identity-centrality component does not change over time, intense positive feelings can change over time in part due to changes to the initial venture idea, role ambiguity, and feedback-seeking behavior (Collewaert, et al., 2016). This suggests that passion, and especially the feelings component of passion, may increase or decrease based on how a person engages with entrepreneurial activities.

We want to emphasize that we do not yet have a lot of conceptual or empirical evidence about how passion emerges, ebbs, and flows during the course of either venture creation or entrepreneurial career development. For example, we do not know if passion is more likely to emerge if individuals are motivated by pull factors (viable opportunities) rather than push factors (necessity entrepreneurs). Some work suggests that pull-motivated entrepreneurship is not necessary for passion to develop, and that push-motivated entrepreneurs can also develop passion (Dalborg & Wincent, 2015), but more research is needed. We lack evidence concerning how resources available to potential entrepreneurs, such as financial or other support from their family members or households (e.g., Pret, et al., 2020), or other sources of support such as from training, accelerator, or incubator programs (discussed below) might impact the speed, intensity, type, or duration of passion development in entrepreneurs. This causes us to ponder whether engagement in all forms of entrepreneurship yields positive feelings of passion, or does this occur only when individuals have optimal conditions around their founding? Do necessity entrepreneurs or those who start firms as a last resort also develop passion for what they are doing? We wonder how various conditions of the founding situation impact the extent to which individuals both develop passionate feelings and internalize founder, entrepreneurial, or other related identities. This is an area ripe for both theoretical and empirical investigation.

In summary, evidence from outside of entrepreneurship suggests that people become more passionate about an activity simply from ongoing engagement in that activity (Mageau, et al., 2009; Vallerand, et al., 2003). Despite having only extremely limited empirical data on this to date, the evidence we do have suggests that entrepreneurial activity may be no different. Regarding entrepreneurial passion and activity engagement, as we noted in Chapter 2, we believe firmly that the centrality of the entrepreneurial identity is an important precursor to, or part of, the development of an entrepreneur's passion, whether in terms of harmonious passion (Murnieks, et al., 2014) or passion for specific entrepreneurial roles such as inventor, founder, or developer (Cardon, et al., 2009, 2013). As such, we implore scholars doing work on passion development to incorporate both development of passionate feelings and development of identity centrality for the target of those feelings into their work.

DEVELOPING PASSION THROUGH EDUCATION

In addition to development through organic activity engagement, entrepreneurial passion may also develop through structured engagement in activities associated with entrepreneurship in a more formalized environment. A common way for individuals to experiment with the possibility of becoming an entrepreneur is to enter a training program or accelerator (Cohen, et al., 2019; Gielnik, et al., 2015). Such programs often provide structured instruction and practice with different activities entrepreneurs must perform in order to be successful. As such, they give aspiring entrepreneurs the chance to "play" with the roles and tasks of being an entrepreneur so that they can develop the necessary skills and assess their true fit with an entrepreneurial career.

Potential or nascent entrepreneurs are often passionate for the *idea* of being an entrepreneur. They might have the entrepreneurial identity as one (of many) potential aspirational identities. Yet, nascent entrepreneurs rarely know what this particular identity actually entails. Their knowledge about what it means to be an entrepreneur comes from the popular press or social media, where famous entrepreneurs are often lauded based on atypical successes (e.g., Jeff Bezos of Amazon; Mark Zuckerberg of Facebook; Elon Musk of Tesla; Bill Gates of Microsoft; Steve Jobs and Steve Wozniak of Apple). In media coverage of entrepreneurs, there is often a heavy survivor bias that favors spectacular, but unusual and idiosyncratic, stories of successful entrepreneurs instead of documenting the numerous unsuccessful or failed ones.

On the other hand, people can learn what it actually takes to be a successful entrepreneur though training programs (Gielnik, et al., 2017; Souitaris, et al., 2007) and accelerator programs (Cohen, et al., 2019), where they are often pushed to do the actual work of an entrepreneur – trying it on for size, if you will – which either helps them realize their aspirational identity and refine their idea of what that identity entails, or helps them realize that the identity is not aligned with their own future goals and ideal self. For example, Markowska, Härtel, Brundin, and Roan (2015) develop a dynamic model of how emotions derived from experiences as aspiring entrepreneurs over time lead to approach or avoidance orientations toward entrepreneurship. Such experiences can happen individually and organically or through formal training or accelerator programs. In such programs, nascent founders experiment with their aspirational identity as entrepreneurs to learn more about what it means to be an entrepreneur, what it takes to be successful in the role, and whether or not that role identity ends up being consistent with their own self-identity. For example, action-oriented entrepreneurship training involves 12 weeks of instruction on different aspects of entrepreneurship where students are subject to active learning and feedback through starting and operating micro businesses (e.g., Gielnik, et al., 2017). Similarly, accelerator programs are typically highly structured cohort-based programs where nascent entrepreneurial teams are given guidance on different aspects of the start-up process and required to engage in product development, customer discovery, and other activities concerning their nascent business idea. Aspiring entrepreneurs are usually provided substantial feedback from instructors and/ or mentors, which helps them assess their capabilities and deficiencies relative to what it takes to be a successful entrepreneur. This process produces emotional reactions to the feedback they are receiving (Cohen, et al., 2019; Markowska, et al., 2015).

While these programs help individuals develop mastery and improve their skills due to the deliberate practice in which they are engaged (Baron & Henry, 2010; Gielnik, et al., 2017), they may not develop entrepreneurial intentions or an entrepreneurial identity, much less entrepreneurial passion. During such processes, nascent entrepreneurs are either "becoming" or "unbecoming," or identifying or dis-identifying as entrepreneurs (Markowska, et al., 2015). The large literatures on identity work (DeRue & Ashford, 2010; Grimes, 2018; Ibarra & Barbulescu, 2010; Pratt, et al., 2006) and identity play (Ibarra & Petriglieri, 2010) help explain the processes through which potential identities might be realized (see also Cohen, et al., 2019, for an explanation specific to entrepreneurship). Entrepreneurial identities are often thought to be crafted (Fauchart & Gruber, 2011; Ibarra & Barbulescu, 2010; Powell & Baker, 2014) such that aspiring entrepreneurs are purposeful about how they turn "who they are" into "who they want to be" (Powell & Baker, 2014) as entrepreneurs.

As with other identity work, when nascent entrepreneurs learn more about what being an entrepreneur actually entails, some will enjoy that work and find it both self-fulfilling and exciting, thus leading to the development of passion (Cohen, et al., 2019; Gielnik, et al., 2015; Souitaris, et al., 2007). For example, a study by Gielnik, Uy, Funken, and Bischoff (2017) found that entrepreneurship training can boost both entrepreneurial self-efficacy and passion in the short term, and that the boost to self-efficacy can help sustain the positive effect of training on passion over a 32-month period. Other people who learn more about what it takes to be a successful entrepreneur through training or an accelerator program, however, will discover that they do not enjoy the reality of being an entrepreneur as much as they enjoyed the idea of it. Instead, they are able to experiment with the entrepreneurial identity and realize that the reality of the identity of "entrepreneur" does not align with their self-identity. For these individuals, entrepreneurial passion will not develop because the identity is a critical component of passion, and they will likely exit such programs with very low intentions to found a venture (Cohen, et al., 2019).

Another possibility is that individuals in such programs will discover which types of entrepreneurial activities or roles they most enjoy and most identify with, which may lead them to construct founding teams for their firms that optimize distinct individual passions (more on team passion in Chapter 6). For example, some individuals may discover that their real passion lies in inventing new products, not in running the business aspects of a new venture (e.g., Cardon, et al., 2009). In this case, they may partner with someone who is more interested in running the venture, while that focal person concentrates on inventing the products or services they sell. One founder of a successful robotics firm told us that he actually had little interest in building a business; his real passion was focused on working with robots, and the inventing and innovation of robotic technology. He pursued venture formation because he saw this as a way to provide funding and resources for his research around robots, but his passion was aimed at inventing, not founding or developing. Conversely, other founders may discover that they love running the actual business, meeting investors, working with clients, and figuring out ways to scale the venture further. Finding complementary passion targets within a team of founders, or at least complementary skills, is a productive outcome of formal training and education programs.

DEVELOPING PASSION THROUGH CONTAGION FROM AND ENGAGEMENT WITH OTHERS

Contagion processes may also help individuals catch the spark of passion, or alter how it grows. While we still need much more research into how these mechanisms work, scholars have theorized that the contagion of passion could be an extremely powerful force (Cardon, 2008). If potential investors and employees can be impacted by contagion processes, so too can entrepreneurs (Murnieks, et al., 2020). Being around others who are engaging in entrepreneurial work can stoke one's own passion fire. For example, taking an entrepreneurship course and being around inspiring professors or other students, alumni, and speakers, can often spark an initial interest that can be nurtured and fanned into a fire to start one's own business. Or, such interaction with other people might create a spark that just smolders beneath the surface of higher wage-paying jobs after graduation for a time before later rekindling into an entrepreneurial intention and/or action.

In studying the dynamics of how other people influence the development and growth of an individual's passion for various activities, Mageau and colleagues (2009) found that social environments providing more autonomy support tended to promote the growth of harmonious versus obsessive passion. The authors also studied the development of passion in children, and found that parents who provided higher levels of autonomy support encouraged development of harmonious passions whereas those who emphasized activity specialization among their children tended to promote development of obsessive passions. While more work needs to be done to confirm these results among different samples, this nevertheless highlights the probability that valued others may play a larger role in the development of our passions than we are currently giving them credit for in the literature.

Recent empirical research in entrepreneurship also emphasizes that the development of passion is an interindividual and social process, rather than something that occurs only intraindividually within a person (Murnieks, et al., 2020). Identities are not only self-defining, but are socially constructed (Stryker & Burke, 2000). As such, interactions with others such as role models, supportive peers or family members, or other people for whom the loss of an entrepreneurial identity would be pivotal, can impact not only the extent to which passion develops, but also the manner in which that passion is internalized (Murnieks, et al., 2020). For example, a recent empirical study found that male entrepreneurs are more likely to experience obsessive passion when they associate the entrepreneurial role with receiving support from important people in their lives, such as family members and friends (Murnieks, et al., 2020). This suggests that this type of support from others may not help male entrepreneurs as much as it may constrain them such that they engage in entrepreneurship out of compulsion due to fear of losing important relationships, instead of joy for engaging in the career or activities associated with it harmoniously. As we will touch on later in Chapter 7, there is much more work that needs to be done to understand both the facilitating and debilitating influences of social support and other factors on the extent and nature of passion development among nascent entrepreneurs.

SOME ADVICE ON STOKING THE FIRES OF PASSION IN OURSELVES AND OTHERS

As educators, our job is both to inspire and to educate – to not only fan the flames of possibilities but also temper them with careful consideration of the reality of what it takes to be successful over the long term. Even though we want to support students' and aspiring entrepreneurs' efforts, we must also give them pointed feedback concerning where they need to revise their strategies, products, skills, behaviors, or attitudes, else we do them a disservice when they go to market and are not prepared for the harsh reality of what it takes to be successful.

In some ways, our role as scholars and educators is like that of firefighters preparing a forest for a controlled burn. Controlled burns are important tools for maintaining the health of a forest, because they consume dead or invasive species that are injurious to the forest, and they help return vital nutrients to the soil that could otherwise take years to decompose (Nationalgeographic.org). Controlled burns also prepare forests to survive and even thrive when hotter, larger, forest fires occur. Firefighters prepare for controlled burns by carefully trimming the vegetation and shaping the terrain in the forest so that when the fire is lit, it only burns in the areas prescribed, and it does not get out of control and consume the entire forest.

Our role as educators is similar: we help students prepare through our feedback, constructive criticism, and education about what happens to passion when it rages out of control. We want students and aspiring founders to experience passion in a controlled manner, such that when their entrepreneurial fire is lit, it burns in the right direction, it burns at the right intensity, and most importantly, it does not burn out of control (consuming resources and areas of their lives that they do not want scorched by its heat). We want entrepreneurial passion to operate like a controlled burn – where it benefits both the individual and everyone around them. But, to do that, our students need educators who are knowledgeable about what the fire of entrepreneurial passion can do (its profits) and what it can harm (its perils) when it is lit.

Given that passion involves one's self-identity and what a person finds personally meaningful, we cannot teach people to be passionate, or force them to find personal meaning in entrepreneurial products, roles, activities, or careers. What we can do is help individuals discover what excites them about entrepreneurship or innovation; help them explore what parts of their hobbies, interests, or social causes are aligned with current or future market needs; and help them understand what it means to be an entrepreneur so they can determine on their own if the reality of an aspirational identity of "entrepreneur" truly aligns with their own self-identity in the present or the future (Cohen, et al., 2019). And of course, our role is to give them the knowledge, experience, and understanding about different parts of the entrepreneurial process so if they choose to pursue this career path they can and will be successful.

6. Passions of entrepreneurs in teams

So far we have written as if there is just one entrepreneur who experiences passion and this passion smolders or flares up to the point where it inspires emotions, cognitions, and actions of that person and those around him or her. This perspective reflects the majority of extant literature, which tends to address entrepreneurial passion as if there is just one central figure (the lead entrepreneur) experiencing that passion (Cardon, et al., 2017c). This is unfortunate, because although we have learned a significant amount about how passion both helps and hinders entrepreneurial progress (as explained in Chapter 4), and where individual entrepreneurial passions might arise (Chapter 5), this body of work ignores the group dynamic that infuses the majority of entrepreneurial firms, which are founded by teams.

Over half of all new firms are founded not by one solitary individual, but rather by a team of entrepreneurs (Kamm, et al., 1990; Klotz, et al., 2014). If passion is such a powerful force for individuals, the obvious question is, therefore, how does passion work within entrepreneurial teams? This is a critical question because, obviously, team dynamics vary drastically from individual decision processes and this likely affects the emergence and functioning of entrepreneurial passion as well. We share an overview of the limited work in this area of research and discuss the multitude of questions for which we still need answers.

HOW PASSION IS DIFFERENT IN NEW VENTURE TEAMS

Although many individuals can be involved in helping a solo entrepreneur found and run a company, firms founded by new venture teams are fundamentally different than sole proprietorships. Such teams have multiple individuals that are actively involved in both the development and the implementation of evolving strategies and ongoing operations of the firm (Klotz, et al., 2014). Team members do not just support a solo entrepreneur, but each person works together such that they are all considered founders of the same organization. This is not a trivial distinction, because being a co-founder involves a different level of commitment and engagement than simply being employed at a startup. Working together as part of a group of founders who have high commitment and engagement, yet potentially conflicting interests and perspectives, creates an environment ripe for conflict and dissention, which can impact, and be impacted by, passion.

When considering individuals working together in teams, the discussion of how passion works gets more complicated (Cardon, et al., 2017c; Chan, 1998). While individuals are still experiencing emotions and cognitions, and demonstrating behaviors as individuals, they are also operating in conjunction with others on venture teams. This creates opportunities for both individual emotions and group emotions to exist (Barsade & Gibson, 1998) and also collective identity-formation processes to occur (Ashforth, et al., 2011; Gioia, et al., 2013). Considering passion in teams leads to possibilities for affective diversity (variation or heterogeneity in individual affective experiences; Barsade & Gibson, 2012; Barsade, et al., 2000; Kaplan, et al., 2009) and identity conflict (disagreements about how the team or its members identify themselves; Ashforth & Mael, 1989; Fauchart & Gruber, 2011; Powell & Baker, 2017) to emerge among team members. The implication is that when examining passion (or any other construct) in teams, we also have to consider team dynamics, processes, and outcomes such as group cohesion, conflict, and needs complementarity.

When moving from an individual to a team-level construct, both conceptualization and measurement of constructs are entirely different (Cardon, et al., 2017c; Chan, 1998). "Conceptually, our interest is no longer just in the level or extent of passion an entrepreneur has, or the focus of that passion, but also in the overlaps and diversity of passions experienced across individual team members" (de Mol, et al., in press, p. 4). Interactions between team members and their own individually held passions raise a number of fascinating questions. Does the passion of individual team members reinforce each other's passions? Do they conflict? What are the outcomes that arise from individual passion synergies or conflicts? Are passions contagious among team members, as they can be to external stakeholders (discussed in Chapter 4)? These are all relevant questions that cannot be answered by considering the passion of individuals alone.

WHAT PASSION IN ENTREPRENEURIAL TEAMS MEANS AND WHAT IT DOES

Thinking about entrepreneurial passion at the team level is more complicated than looking at it within individuals. In teams, there are several different ways to conceptualize and study passion. First, we could look at the passion held individually by each team member, and then aggregate those measurements into an average level of passion within the team. Second, acknowledging that differences in passion levels or targets between individuals might be meaningful, we could instead study the configuration of the passions experienced between individual team members and analyze their homogeneity or heterogeneity. Third, we could investigate the possibility that a new type of shared passion might emerge at the team level that is entirely different in type and constitution from the individual-level passions of each entrepreneur (Cardon, et al., 2017c). Cardon, Post, and Forster (2017c) provide a rich explanation of these different ways passion can be looked at within teams as well as a dynamic conceptual model of how team passions might form (bottom-up processes from individuals to teams) and inform key outcomes (top-down processes from teams to individual and organizational outcomes). We do not wish to repeat their arguments here, but instead highlight the divergent ways passion might be looked at in teams, as well as the limited empirical findings to date.

Average Team Passion

Perhaps the simplest way to examine how passion might operate within entrepreneurial teams is to look at the average level of passion among team members (i.e., the mean of individual-level passions), acknowledging that each person's passion may differ for different targets. This suggests that scholars need to create an average team passion score for each target or domain, such as inventing, founding, or developing. Recent empirical work suggests that average team passion has a positive effect on team performance, measured as the quality of the business idea the team pursues (de Mol, et al., in press).

Team Passion Diversity

That said, looking at an average level for any team construct is problematic if you do not also consider the dispersion of individuals around that average (de Jong & Dirks, 2012). In other words, it likely matters if you have some team members who are highly passionate for a set of activities (e.g., founding) while others are not passionate at all about those activities (e.g., some are highly passionate about founding while others are not passionate about founding at all), versus a team in which all members are only moderately passionate about the same set of activities (Drnovsek, et al., 2009). What matters is both how passionate team members are (high vs. low) and the targets of their different levels of passion (highly passionate for what?). For example, looking at some data gathered for a recent project on team passion, we noted that one company failure was attributed to the company having "two heads" – where one founder was highly passionate about technology and the other was highly passionate about the business side of the firm. One of those founders said, "The problem was … when it came time to make hard decisions the two-headed structure really didn't work" (Ehrenberg, 2008; de Mol, et al., in press, p. 6). In this case, both founders were highly passion-ate, but for different targets (technology vs. the business). This can be especially problematic if there are resource constraints and disagreements among team members about how, where, or when to invest resources in different aspects of the business (e.g., developing new products vs. growing the market for existing products). Similarly, conflicts can easily arise from some team members being highly passionate about the firm's growth while others are not passionate about that growth, or anything else related to the business. This typically occurs in situations where a firm is doing well and one partner wants to reinvest firm profits in growing the business further, while another partner wants to withdraw those profits from the firm for personal enjoyment.

Average Team Passion and Team Passion Diversity

Because of these concerns, it is essential to examine average team passion in conjunction with the dispersion or diversity of individual passions within the team. Organizational behavior research indicates that affective diversity can lead to higher task and relational conflict, as well as lower cooperation among team members (Barsade, et al., 2000), and identity conflict can be problematic for team performance (Fauchart & Gruber, 2011) and the ability for the team to stay together

(Powell & Baker, 2017). This implies diversity in passion could also present challenges in teams. Based on the work of Harrison and Klein (2007), Cardon, Post, and Forster (2017c) conceptualize team passion diversity as having two dimensions: *passion focus variety* and *passion intensity separation*. Passion focus variety is "a measure of how different members of the team are concerning the specific roles or objects for which they feel passion" (p. 289). Passion focus variety concentrates on differences in the specific targets about which each team member is passionate (e.g., one department member is strongly passionate about teaching, while the another is highly passionate about research). Passion intensity separation involves "the dispersion in the level of activation of emotion experienced by team members" (p. 289) or how passionate each team member is (e.g., one team member is highly passionate about the project while another is not at all passionate about it). Both types of diversity within an entrepreneurial team may be an important catalyst for or detriment to cohesive team operations and outcomes.

Empirical work by de Mol and colleagues (in press) shows that once you consider passion diversity along with average levels of passion within a team, the average level of passion becomes non-significant in predicting the quality of the business ideas generated in the short term. Indeed, their findings reveal that while overall average team passion has no significant effect, diversity in terms of intensity separation is harmful to the quality of business ideas generated. Intensity separation among team members in (1) their passion for founding the firm and (2) their passion for developing it is especially harmful to the ability of the team to generate a high-quality business idea. In addition, while focus variety did not impact evaluations of the quality of business ideas generated, there was a significant negative effect of passion focus variety on later venture performance (de Mol, et al., in press). It appears that teams that experience greater passion diversity (in terms of both focus variety and intensity separation) experience worse short- and long-term performance than teams without such passion diversity among team members, regardless of the overall average level of their individual passions. In short, passion diversity really matters in teams.

Team Entrepreneurial Passion (TEP)

A different way of looking at passion within entrepreneurial teams is to examine their shared passions. Cardon, Post, and Forster (2017c, p. 288) develop a construct called team entrepreneurial passion (TEP), reflecting the "level of shared intense positive feelings for a collective team identity that is high in identity-centrality for the new venture team" (p. 286), which is "independent from individual team members' identities or emotions." TEP represents what we, as a team, are passionate about, and the extent of that passion. For example, at Clarks (the British shoe company), "Our passion is to listen to our customers and deliver a product that allows the consumer to feel the pride, respect and trust of everyone at the Clarks Companies N.A." (Achievers.com, 2016). Annies.com is passionate about "food, people, and the planet we all share" (Annies.com, 2015). These cases illustrate collective, versus individual, views of passion. TEP is measured by asking team members what the team, as a team, is passionate about, and to what extent, rather than asking each team member about their individual passions.

Just as individual passion can be focused on different objects, TEP can be focused on a single object or multiple different objects. While Cardon, Post, and Forster (2017c) conceptualized monofocal (one object) versus polyfocal (multiple objects) TEP, Santos and Cardon (2019) expanded this conceptualization to examine both incomplete polyfocal TEP (multiple but not all passion domains are represented in the team's shared passion) and complete polyfocal TEP (all passion domains are represented in the team's shared passion). For example, a monofocal TEP of a new venture team would exist when the team is passionate about growth, and not passionate about inventing new products or services or the product they sell, specifically. A polyfocal TEP would exist when a new venture team is passionate about all aspects of the entrepreneurial process, such as inventing, founding, and developing the firm.

Empirical results from Santos and Cardon (2019) indicate that not all new venture teams experience a state of TEP, or collective positive emotions for a shared identity. This is interesting because it highlights that a unified passion may not emerge in all cases. While most teams in their sample experienced shared positive emotions for entrepreneurial activities, many did not share "a common understanding of the identity of the team around those activities" (Santos & Cardon, 2019, p. 496). Cardon, Post, and Forster (2017c) note that TEP is unlikely to form unless there is at least one member of the team with at least a moderate amount of passion, since individual members' affective states are important stimuli in the creation of a collective affective tone (Bartel & Saavedra, 2000; Sy, et al., 2005). This is noteworthy because it reinforces the idea that for a passion fire to burn, someone needs to provide that initial hot spark. TEP may also be unlikely to form if there is a high level of turnover of members within the team (Cardon, et al., 2017c). We speculate here that the fire of passion requires continuity, otherwise it dies from lack of maintenance. Someone has to tend to the fire and keep it burning. Importantly, teams that did not experience TEP in Santos and Cardon's study (2019) had the worst performance, consistent with research demonstrating that founding teams with incongruent (competing and incompatible) identities have trouble making forward progress with their venture (Powell & Baker, 2017).

For teams that did experience TEP, performance was maximized when that TEP represented all domains (e.g., inventing, founding, developing) of the entrepreneurial process (complete polyfocal TEP), and was at its worst when TEP was polyfocal but incomplete (representing some but not all sets of activities involved in the entrepreneurial process) (Santos & Cardon, 2019). This suggests that in terms of team passion, new venture teams are best served by creating shared positive and intense emotions for a common identity that includes all aspects of the process (e.g., inventing, founding, and developing).

A recent study of TEP found that its relationship with performance depends on whether the team's passion focus is aligned with the development stage of the venture (Boone, et al., in press). More specifically, in the conceptualization stage, teams experience less relationship conflict when they experience monofocal TEP for inventing or polyfocal TEP for inventing and founding, but have higher relationship conflict when they experience monofocal TEP for founding. In other words, teams that are collectively passionate about inventing, or collectively passionate about both inventing and founding, fare better during the conceptualization stage of their business. For teams in the commercialization stage, TEP for inventing continues to reduce relationship conflict, but in this stage, TEP for founding also reduces relationship conflict, and both types of monofocal TEP enhance team performance (although these effects are not linear; Boone, et al., in press). In addition, during the commercialization stage, polyfocal TEP is better than either monofocal TEP for founding or monofocal TEP for inventing in terms of its effects on team performance (Boone, et al., in press). In other words, start-up teams in the commercialization stage fare better when the team is passionate about both inventing products or services and founding the firm, rather than when the team is passionate about either set of activities alone.

Although the processes through which such shared TEP might evolve have been conceptualized theoretically (Cardon, et al., 2017c; Santos and Cardon, 2019), empirical study of different potential methods of TEP creation is lacking. This is an important oversight in the literature given the emergent findings that TEP offers both short- and long-term performance benefits for a new venture team. Taken together, these results suggest that the effects of a team's shared passion (TEP) depend on the specific nature of that passion (whether it has one target or multiple targets, and which targets) as well as the extent to which that focus is aligned with the stage of development the venture is in at that time.

RESEARCH QUESTIONS ABOUT PASSION IN ENTREPRENEURIAL TEAMS RIPE FOR FURTHER STUDY

While the conceptual and empirical work discussed above has advanced our understanding of how passion might work in entrepreneurial teams in important ways, a vast number of questions remain. We focus on the largest gaps in existing knowledge and opportunities for future research, but note that many others exist.

First, we know nothing about how other team dynamics influence how passion forms within teams or the impact of that passion. For example, does passion in a start-up team initiate from one passionate person who pulls others into their start-up venture? If so, do those new team members also get ignited with the spark of passion, such that their own individual passion for the venture or other targets grows? As noted in Chapter 4, passion can be contagious to external stakeholders (e.g., Breugst, et al., 2012; Cardon, 2008), but how do such contagion processes work within founding teams? Given the amplified levels of commitment and engagement between founders (vs. employees), does the contagion process operate differently? How does the extent to which added team members feel passion impact team dynamics and/or firm outcomes? Is it better for the team or firm to have a group of passionate people initially, or a team of skilled people that eventually develop passion? Does it matter if it is the lead entrepreneur who is the most passionate, or can it be a team member with less formal power that drives the emotional energy of the team; does this prevent the lead entrepreneur from burning out? How does team size impact the dynamics or outcomes of average team passion, team passion diversity, or TEP development? How do team processes such as shared mental models, conflict management, or communication patterns influence passion development or outcomes?

Second, as this long list of questions clearly indicates, we need process-based longitudinal work that explores passion dynamics within founding teams. Ideally, observation and data collection would start before teams even form by examining the passions of individuals who later become members of a founding team. Great contexts for this work would be rapid start-up weekends or courses or entrepreneurship centers that facilitate team creation for founding where budding, emergent, nascent firms start to form and more quickly add and shed members as they figure out who and what they need as part of the founding team. Similar to Powell and Baker's work on the creation and destruction of founding team identities (2017), researchers could examine passion layered on top of those identities to determine how individual passion levels and objects come together within teams (or don't), how TEP forms (or doesn't), and with what consequences before, during, and after team formation and throughout venture launch, growth, and ultimate exit, whether productive or not (Wennberg, et al., 2010).

As part of future research on passion within teams, we encourage scholars to expand their individual conceptualizations of passion (noted in chapters 2 and 3) to groups and teams. For example, as discussed in Chapter 3, there are many potential targets of entrepreneurial passion for individuals and teams, yet extant studies of passion in teams have used the original three domains developed in Cardon, Wincent, Singh, and Drnovsek (2009). New research needs to incorporate other targets of passion in examining individual passion(s), average passion and passion diversity within teams, and collective TEP.

Further, to our knowledge there has been no work on team passion from the conceptual perspective of the DMP, which is surprising. We anticipate this to be a rich area for further insights. What happens when some team members experience harmonious passion while others experience obsessive passion for activities in which the team is engaged? If one team member is obsessively passionate, does this help or hinder team processes or outcomes? Research in the project management domain suggests that leaders who possess obsessive passion for their projects can positively influence goal attainment for the team (Omorede, et al., 2013). While this finding alludes to interesting team effects, we still know little about how the Dualistic Model of Passion (DMP) operates in team contexts. For example, does it create perceptions of inequity among team members if the obsessively passionate person has trouble disengaging from work while more harmoniously passionate team members are able to balance their work for the venture with other activities in their lives? We are unaware of any research on the DMP, either in the entrepreneurship context or otherwise, concerning how harmonious and obsessive passions work within teams working toward a common goal, and we strongly encourage such investigation.

Given that entrepreneurs do not operate in isolation, but instead work largely within teams and with a variety of stakeholders such as customers, employees, suppliers, and funders, developing a better understanding of the dynamics and impacts of passion emergence, contagion, operation, and dispersion within founding teams is essential.

7. Opportunities for future research on passion and entrepreneurship

Over the past decade, there has been a virtual explosion in research surrounding entrepreneurial passion; the number of peer-reviewed academic articles on passion and entrepreneurship has grown over 500 percent from 2009 to 2019. This abundance of conceptual and empirical work has shed light into the many ways in which passion is embedded in the entrepreneurial process. We liken this work to a bright fire burning in the night. Each paper adds additional fuel to this fire and extends the light; it makes the fire grow bigger and brighter and illuminates more of the entrepreneurial passion realm. That said, as the light expands, so does the number and magnitude of additional questions we can and should be asking about this phenomenon. Each paper adds to our knowledge, but also raises new questions and offers new ways of thinking about passion and entrepreneurship. In this chapter, we think forward by discussing different arenas of research that still lie unexplored and that are beckoning us to uncover and examine them. We also comment on best practices and our recommendations for doing this work.

PROVIDING GREATER THEORETICAL AND METHODOLOGICAL PRECISION

As entrepreneurial passion research accumulates, we have noticed a growing trend toward expanding the term "passion." In Chapter 2, we outlined the primary theories that have been used to study entrepreneurial passion as well as a number of other different conceptualizations of the construct. At this juncture in time, we believe that as a body of scholars, we need to be more precise about our usage of the term "passion." We need to be specific about whether we are studying the actual, self-reported experience of passion (e.g., Cardon, et al., 2013; Murnieks, et al., 2014) compared to the perceived display of entrepreneurial passion (Mitteness, et al., 2012), or displays (Cardon, et al., 2017b; Chen, et al., 2009) or experiences (Gielnik, et al., 2015) of overall enthusiasm without an identity component. Some scholars have been explicit about differences such as these (e.g., Breugst, et al., 2012), whereas other studies tend to equate the construct of passion with animated expressions and body movements. Intrinsic motivation and positive affect can also drive the latter, so we need to be careful about equating passion with these types of measurements too leniently. Entrepreneurial passion is not the same thing as enthusiasm or energetic presentations because passion possesses deep ties to one's identity. Entrepreneurial passion scholars have taken great pains to distinguish how passion is special and unique from motivation and affect, so it behooves us to carry that precision over into our definitions and our measurements as we move forward.

As scholars deeply embedded in the study of passion, we have both had numerous conversations at conferences with our fellow psychology, organizational behavior, and management colleagues who question the uniqueness of entrepreneurial passion compared to motivation or emotion. If we are not precise about our usage of the construct, we run the risk of polluting it, and jeopardizing its credibility. This is not to say that one definition or conceptualization of passion is correct (say, the EP model or the Dualistic Model of Passion, DMP) while others are not. We are not trying to exclude or denigrate new conceptualizations. On the contrary, we applaud more theoretical work surrounding the actual construction and analysis of the core construct of passion, both in entrepreneurship and in other work and non-work contexts. That said, we argue that it is important to be precise about what is being called passion in future work, and also to be precise about the conceptualization being employed to delineate how that conceptualization differs from current theory and why these differences are important. Authors concerned with both EP and the DMP have worked diligently to distinguish passion from extant motivational and affective constructs. Any other conceptualization of passion should strive to highlight these differentiating factors as well.

DEEPER THEORETICAL DEVELOPMENT

As Table 1.1 indicates, the majority of the work surrounding passion has been empirical in nature. This highlights some glaring gaps in our theories of entrepreneurial passion. We have quite limited knowledge of how passion ebbs and flows over time for entrepreneurs, or how it changes dynamically such as moving from obsessive to harmonious, or vice versa, or shifting targets over time, such as from inventing to founding to developing. Theoretically, we don't know if or how such changes might occur, what social or environmental factors might prompt those changes, or what might be the implications for outcomes of interest, such as those we discussed in Chapter 4. Moreover, how is entrepreneurial passion affected by a number of signature events that we know are prevalent in the entrepreneurial context such as exogenous shocks (environmental catastrophes or economic changes) or important firm events (venture capital investment, initial public offerings, or liquidation of the venture)? Further, while some researchers have suggested that different targets of passion may be more salient at different stages of firm development (e.g., Cardon, et al., 2009), empirical evidence to this effect has not yet emerged. Empirical studies have provided an indication that stages of development and large exogenous and firm events might impact passion, but we need more comprehensive theoretical models that explain how and why passion changes across time, and with what effects. We encourage conceptual and empirical work on these possibilities that integrates research on identity development and reconciliation of multiple potentially competing identities (e.g., congruent and incongruent identities; Powell & Baker, 2014), as well as recent findings on the implications of shifting entrepreneurial role identities over time (Mathias & Williams, 2018).

INTEGRATION OF THEORIES

Throughout this book, we have discussed the prevalence of two main theories of passion: EP (Cardon, et al., 2009) and the DMP (Vallerand, et al., 2003). We have noted repeatedly that these two theories are not mutually exclusive. Whereas EP focuses on passion tied to specific role identities within the entrepreneurial domain (e.g., inventing, founding, developing, and others), the DMP concentrates on the type of passion experienced (e.g., harmonious and obsessive). Despite these different foci, it is entirely possible for an entrepreneur to be obsessively passionate about inventing new products, or for a founder to be harmoniously passionate about developing their venture. Given this, we need more work that integrates the theories of entrepreneurial passion.

Further, more and more scholarship is emerging surrounding displays of passion and how these displays are perceived by various stakeholders such as employees (Breugst, et al., 2012), a variety of investors (Chen, et al., 2009), angel investors (Mitteness, et al., 2012), and crowdfunders (Li, et al., 2017). Work such as this could integrate either EP or the DMP to analyze how passion experienced by the entrepreneur for specific role identities or harmonious/obsessive passion aligns with or contradicts displays of passion and/or perceptions of passion by stakeholders. Ultimately, research should examine how experiences, displays, and perceptions of passion align or don't and how that (mis)alignment influences those stake-holders. Some scholars have already embarked on integrating these theories (e.g., Huyghe, et al., 2016), but more research that does this is needed.

We also need work that examines the emotional labor of the entrepreneur and how they can and cannot translate the passions they experience into passionate displays that are per-ceived by others to be authentic (e.g., Mitteness, et al., 2012). Examining the toll of such emotional labor in terms of time spent developing display skills, well-being costs that result from having to display what one does not feel or suppress display of what one does feel, and training costs from pro-viding guidance on emotional displays, is needed. Additional research comparing the potential advantages that different types of emotional displays may or may not lead to would also be valuable (Cardon, et al., 2017b).

CONSIDERING THE SOCIAL CONSTRUCTION OF IDENTITIES AND THEREFORE PASSIONS

In Chapters 2 and 3, we discussed the importance of identity for passion. Identities are core elements that establish the foundation for passions because they relate a profound love for an object to one's self-concept. We must remember that identities are social constructs that bridge one's own sense of self with how others see us. Identity theory explicitly recog-nizes the consideration for other people's viewpoints and how their reactions can influence identity construction, motivation, and self-construal (Burke, 1991; Stryker & Burke, 2000). This has important implications for the development of passion. More specifically, if an entrepreneur's identity construction is influenced by the actions and reactions of other people, then it stands to reason that their entrepreneurial passion should be as well.

While work on the development of passion is somewhat sparse in general, the research that does exist already highlights the fact that other people influence the development and growth of an individual's passion. For example, Mageau and colleagues (2009) found that environments providing more autonomy support foster harmonious versus obsessive passion. Similarly, Murnieks, Cardon, and Haynie (2020) found that entrepreneurs who experience higher levels of affective interpersonal commitment (affect associated with important relationships that may be damaged given the loss of an identity) are more likely to develop stronger feelings of obsessive passion. These papers highlight that the development of entrepreneurial passion is likely not a purely intraindividual process. Instead, as we discussed in Chapter 5, social environments and other stakeholders influence the formation of passion in entrepreneurs.

Important questions in this realm remain. For example, in entrepreneurship, what role do close others play in the development of passions? Do parents or spouses have especially important roles in how passion develops? What about other entrepreneurs? We know that mentoring and networking groups like the Young Entrepreneurs' Organization (YEO) can play important functions in supporting founders. Given the heavy social and identity influence groups like this can have on an entrepreneur, it stands to reason that they might also affect entrepreneurial passion. While some research exists on how entrepreneurial passion affects entrepreneurial networks (e.g., Ho & Pollack, 2014), we know very little about how networks affect the development and sustenance of entrepreneurial passion.

As passion scholars, we need to pay more attention to the interindividual influences in the development of passion. Entrepreneurship itself is a social process, and we need to understand how social forces can play critical roles in the formation of passion. We predict that understanding these influences will become even more imperative in the near future.

Digital and communication technology continues to increase at an exponential rate. Smartphones and social media applications allow entrepreneurs to be connected to more and more people every day. Each new connection, each new impression, each new social media post scanned by an entrepreneur on Facebook, YouTube, Instagram, Twitter, or Snapchat provides an input for his or her identity. Increased social media elevates the exposure to the actions and impressions left by valued others as well as prominent and popular entrepreneurs such as Elon Musk, Jeff Bezos, or Mark Zuckerberg. How do all these impressions influence one's entrepreneurial identity, and by extension, one's entrepreneurial passion? In the future, will social media play a larger role in shaping entrepreneurial identities, and driving entrepreneurial passion? Will social media change the way in which entrepreneurs communicate their passions to stakeholders, and with what effects? These trends beckon us to investigate further.

INCORPORATING BOTH PERSONALITY AND PASSION

While we are explicit about the nature of passion as a state (and not a trait), we actually know very little about how entrepreneurial passion interacts with other personality traits. For example, do conscientious entrepreneurs tend to exert even more effort when they feel passionate? Do other personality factors like openness to experience or emotional stability moderate the effect of entrepreneurial passion on effort or performance? Is it possible that personality moderates the effect of passion contagion on a venture's employees or other key stakeholders? When potential investors view an entrepreneur who is passionate, do they increase their evaluations if the entrepreneur is also conscientious or extraverted (e.g., Murnieks, et al., 2016)? Or, do they discount the effect of entrepreneurial passion on their evaluations if they perceive the entrepreneur is not agreeable or is neurotic? A host of research has looked at the influence of personality and other enduring characteristics of entrepreneurs (e.g., Rauch & Frese, 2007; Zhao & Seibert, 2006; Zhao, et al., 2010), and the time has come to integrate that work with our work on entrepreneurial passion to learn more about their marginal contributions and combined, as well as possibly conflicting, effects.

LONGITUDINAL WORK

One of the most vital areas in need of greater exploration surrounds more robust study designs. The vast majority of research in the field of entrepreneurial passion to date has been cross-sectional in nature and based on self-reported and other-reported survey data. Given that numerous authors have proposed the idea that entrepreneurial passion may not operate in a linear fashion, but rather in reciprocal loops, we need more longitudinal work. Various studies have shown that passion is both an antecedent to and a consequent from other constructs such as self-efficacy (Cardon & Kirk, 2015; Murnieks, et al., 2014) and effort (Gielnik, et al., 2015; Murnieks, et al., 2014). It is likely both. We know that positive affect can result from important interactions at work (e.g., affective events theory; Weiss & Cropanzano, 1996) and also influence subsequent outcomes. It is likely that passion operates in a similar manner. These reinforcing and reciprocal loops may explain how passion develops over time, and why it carries as much force and perseverance as we suspect and have started to uncover. Although many scholars have suggested this may be the manner in which entrepreneurial passion works, to date, longitudinal analyses to confirm these effects are sparse. We are sympathetic to the challenges of conducting longitudinal studies with large samples of entrepreneurs in the field, and with trying to capture or manipulate passion in experimental designs. Nevertheless, the time has come for more of this kind of work if we are to advance our understanding of passion in a rigorous manner.

We also encourage dynamic multilevel models concerning the likely reciprocal influences between firm outcomes and the passion of entrepreneurs. To what extent does the success of the firm drive passion versus passion driving the success of the firm, and how might that change over time? How do early success signals (e.g., at the end of an accelerator program) fuel or solidify passion formation? Given that firm and individual identities are often intertwined for entrepreneurs (Shepherd & Haynie, 2009), examining the mutual influences of firm occurrences and outcomes with entrepreneurial passion ebbs and flows seems promising.

UNCOVERING MECHANISMS FOR PASSION'S INFLUENCE

To date, the majority of entrepreneurial passion research has focused on the outcomes that passion drives. In Chapter 4, we discussed a myriad of beneficial (profits) as well as detrimental (perils) consequences that can result from entrepreneurial passion. This research has opened new frontiers in helping us understand what impact passion might have on other important constructs and outcomes in the entrepreneurial process. However, as a body of scholars, we have spent considerably less time examining the mechanisms by which entrepreneurial passion might drive these outcomes. Namely, we do not know the extent to which entrepreneurial passion is a proximal or distal component in driving behaviors and performance; we do not have a deep understanding of the mediators that might operate in between entrepreneurial passion and behavior.

From the sparse work that does exist in this area, there are indications that entrepreneurial passion's effect on consequential outcomes may not be direct. For example, Huyghe, Knockaert, and Obschonka (2016) found that entrepreneurial self-efficacy mediates the influence of entrepreneurial passion on spin-off/start-up intentions among university researchers aspiring to start new ventures based on their scientific work. They also found that affective organizational commitment mediates the relationship between obsessive scientific passion and spin-off/start-up intentions for this same group of people. Mueller, Wolfe, and Syed (2017) found that the influence of entrepreneurial passion for developing a venture on venture performance is mediated by locomotion, assessment, and grit. Drnovsek, Cardon, and Patel (2016) found that the impact of entrepreneurial passion for developing on venture growth is partially mediated by goal commitment.

Taken together, these studies and others provide evidence that the linkages between entrepreneurial passion and both individual- and firm-level outcomes are mediated by other important constructs. This should not be surprising to us given that in the original theoretical conception of entrepreneurial passion, Cardon, Wincent, Singh, and Drnovsek (2009) propose numerous pathways between passion and individual as well as firm outcomes that are mediated by goal-related and cognitive variables. Yet, research has generally neglected the examination of these intervening pathways. At this point in the evolution of this stream of research, it is too convenient and too simplistic to argue that entrepreneurial passion has direct effects on important outcomes. We need to start conducting more intensive research aimed at understanding the complex mediated and moderated pathways through which entrepreneurial passion works within the venturing process.

EXPANDING THE NOMOLOGICAL NET

In Chapter 2, we emphasized the point that entrepreneurial passion is distinct from related constructs such as intrinsic motivation and positive affect. Numerous scholars who have theorized about the nature of passion have been adamant in explicating how it is different and unique from similar constructs in the motivational and affective spheres (e.g., Cardon, et al., 2009, 2013; Jachimowicz, et al., 2019; Murnieks, et al., 2014; Vallerand, et al., 2003; Vallerand, 2015). While we think that the singular and special nature of entrepreneurial passion has been established, we still believe that more work is needed to understand what this unique essence means. Specifically, we suggest that more research is needed that includes entrepreneurial passion as well as variables capturing intrinsic motivation and positive affect to understand how much incremental variance the former explains. Most empirical work that models entrepreneurial passion does not control for the variance attributable to intrinsic motivation and positive affect. Thus, while we know that the experience of entrepreneurial passion does significantly predict behavior, we do not know how much more it explains above and beyond other well-studied affective and motivational constructs. Moving forward, passion scholars need to make a point of incorporating more control variables so that we do not overstate the influence of entrepreneurial passion on outcomes.

EXPLORING SELF-REGULATION OF PASSION

We have noted previously that entrepreneurial passion is not a trait; passion is not a genetic component of one's personality (see Chapter 2 for more detail on this point). Rather, it is a state: an affective, motivational component tied to one's identity that can be developed (and can wane) over time. If it can be changed, it stands to reason that it can also be managed and regulated. We argue that one of the most exciting implications of the emerging research on the dynamic nature of passion is that it can (and perhaps should) be self-regulated by the individual who occupies the center of the entrepreneurial passion experience: the entrepreneur. For example, a deep literature exists around affective/emotion regulation (e.g., Gross, 1999, 2015) and the various strategies by which it can be applied (e.g., Naragon-Gainey, et al., 2017). Similarly, prominent motivation theories such as self-determination theory (e.g., Deci & Ryan, 1985; Ryan & Deci, 2000) and goal theory (e.g., Locke & Latham, 1990, 2002) acknowledge the importance of processes of self-regulation involving the assessment and achievement of desired objectives and states of being. In short, both affective and motivation theorists highlight the critical role that self-regulation plays in affective and motivational processes.

Moreover, numerous identity scholars who talk about identity work (e.g., Ashforth & Kreiner, 1999), identity processes (e.g., Burke, 1991), and identity construction (e.g., Dutton, et al., 2010), discuss the agentic nature by which individuals develop, manage, and interact with their identities. Identities are a core component of passion, and these identity scholars all emphasize that identities can be managed and self-regulated. If identities, motivations, and affect can all be self-regulated, it stands to reason that passions should be as well.

Interestingly, EP was developed using self-regulation theory as the overarching conceptual framework. Cardon, Wincent, Singh, and Drnovsek (2009, p. 518) argue that "when a particular identity is activated (say, *inventor*), we expect that the experience of passion mobilizes an entrepreneur's self-regulation processes that are directed toward effectiveness in the pursuit of the corresponding entrepreneurial goal." Yet, up to this point, most research tends to look at entrepreneurial passion as something that develops as a result of social forces (e.g., Murnieks, et al., 2020) or intraindividually (e.g., Gielnik, et al., 2015) but does not take an agentic view of it. Despite early writings noting the importance of self-regulation processes, we as a field are not viewing passion as a construct that can and should be consciously developed and managed. Given that passion can result in both profits and perils, we should manage it. We should attempt to maximize the profits and avoid the perils. We need more research on how entrepreneurs can do so, and with what effects.

ADDRESSING MEASUREMENT ISSUES

Most work to date has been survey based, whether self-reported or other-reported. This is often appropriate, but also raises concerns about which we need to be mindful. For instance, asking questions about passion may include social desirability effects concerning how much passion an entrepreneur "should" have or demonstrate. In addition, certain individuals (perhaps those lower in emotional intelligence) may be unaware of the degree to which they promote/project their entrepreneurial passion to others. Given that more robust methodologies are becoming available to address these concerns, we need to be more proactive in using these tools. For example, facial analysis (Stroe, et al., in press), voice analysis (Allison, et al., 2018), and textual analysis (Letwin, et al., 2016) are ways of discerning passion that do not require reports from individuals. We need to begin conducting more research that analyzes the degree of correspondence between one's self-reports of entrepreneurial passion and its facial, vocal, or written displays. These tools can help us achieve those objectives.

It is also time for us to expand our methodologies to utilize much newer technologies to better understand processes involving passion of entrepreneurs. As a feeling, passion is an enduring emotional reaction attributed to a specific stimulus that requires effortful processing, storing, and retrieval in one's brain (Schwarz & Clore, 2007). As such, we should be able to find evidence of passion stored in neural processing units of the brain and therefore to utilize fMRI (functional magnetic resonance imaging) technology to study those patterns of brain activation associated with passionate feelings. Passion should also evidence itself as a state of activation when entrepreneurs' feelings are salient, which can be observable through galvanic skin responses and other biophysical reactions of the entrepreneur. Accordingly, we should be able to observe the extent of an entrepreneur's passion for different targets through use of technology such as the Empatica

E4, which is a wearable device similar to a wrist-watch that tracks emotional activation and increased cognitive workload through electrodermal activity of one's skin.

Also, just as we noted above that we need to be more precise in our conceptualization of passion, we suggest that we need to be more mindful of ensuring that our chosen conceptualization and theoretical approaches are aligned with our methodologies and measurement. One should not conceptualize passion using EP's focus on specific sub-roles as targets and then use Vallerand's DMP measure (Vallerand, et al., 2003). Similarly, if one's research interest is the manner in which passion is internalized into one's identity, whether harmoniously or obsessively, then using the EP scales (Cardon, et al., 2013) to measure this does not make sense.

SCREENING FOR THE PROMISE OF PASSION DEVELOPMENT

Given that we know entrepreneurial passion can drive important outcomes related to effort and perseverance, how do we find it? This is a relevant question for a number of different stakeholders in the entrepreneurship process, including investors. Investors have shown both through their own espoused preferences (e.g., Murnieks, et al., 2016) and through their actual decisions (e.g., Warnick, et al., 2018) that entrepreneurial passion can be an attractive quality of entrepreneurs. We also know that entrepreneurial passion can drive important behaviors related to effort and perseverance (e.g., Cardon & Kirk, 2015). But we lack forward-looking instruments that anticipate the development of passion. All of our current measurement scales assess the presence of passion once it exists. Moreover, the assessment of passion in the field is often done tacitly and idiosyncratically by practitioners who follow the "I'll know it when I see it" heuristic.

We need more reliable ways to gauge the conditions under which passion is likely to develop, and the people who are likely to experience it. We need to develop theory and methods for predicting the development of this powerful characteristic. This is necessary because we are also seeing emerging evidence for situations where one type of passion is beneficial, and another may be problematic (e.g., Breugst, et al., 2012; Ho & Pollack, 2014). Finding ways to predict the development of the types of entrepreneurial passion that are best suited for given contexts might help key stakeholders refine their venture investment decision-making.

FINAL ADVICE FOR STUDYING PASSION IN ENTREPRENEURSHIP (OR OUTSIDE OF IT)

Throughout this book, we have highlighted what we believe to be the more prevalent trends that have emerged in the entrepreneurial passion literature. The expansive growth in this stream offers much promise; however, we have also seen practices that we consider to be perilous if we, as a body of scholars, are not thoughtful and precise about how we conduct research. Herein, we offer our opinions on some of the more important elements to consider as we continue to study passion.

First, we need to be clear about the particular conceptualization of entrepreneurial passion we purport to theorize about and study. As we discussed in Chapter 2, is the conceptualization being employed (EP, DMP, or otherwise) properly paired with the theoretical basis of the construct (emotion vs. motivation), as well as the measurement (degree of passion experienced vs. the type of internalization)? We also need to be careful to distinguish passion from other related constructs such as positive affect, enthusiasm, or intrinsic motivation.

Second, what is the target of entrepreneurial passion in the study (see Chapter 3)? Is it a set of activities or something else? What identity is reflected in the target of the passion under examination? Is this identity a general one (entrepreneur), a specific one (inventing), or non-entrepreneurial in nature (hobby, etc.)? What implications might the identity related to the target have on the study? Are we allowing for individuals to have multiple targets of passion or for different amounts of passion for different targets? We need to be clear on the target(s) of passion in our research and potentially to allow for multiple targets to evaluate their independent and interdependent origins and effects.

Third, we need to be mindful about the modality of passion in the study. Are we studying experienced passion or displayed passion? For both types, how is the identity centrality of passion being assessed? How do we know that the affective/motivational construct that is being captured is actually passion, versus intrinsic motivation or positive affect or enthusiasm?

Finally, as noted above, while we encourage future research that continues to examine the outcomes (see Chapter 4) and antecedents (see Chapter 5) of passion, we especially encourage work that goes beyond simply linear models to consider dynamic, longitudinal, multilevel, and contextualized conceptual and empirical models of passion, both within the entrepreneurship context and in other work and life contexts.

8. Concluding thoughts on passion and entrepreneurship

We have each spent more than fifteen years studying passions of entrepreneurs, sometimes in joint projects, and sometimes not. Our goal in this book was to provide readers with an in-depth understanding of the theoretical and conceptual advancements and findings to date concerning passion and entrepreneurship. As we explained in Chapter 2, although there are different conceptualizations of entrepreneurial passion, the consensus in the field is that passion involves intense feelings and motivations for deeply held identities, passion is target specific, and passions motivate thinking and actions toward (rather than away from) their target. As we noted in Chapter 3, passion can be oriented toward very different targets, including high-level social and professional roles (such as being an entrepreneur), specific activity-based sets of roles (such as inventing, founding, and developing), object- or hobby-specific roles (such as backpacking or a specific product or service), social causes (such as alleviating hunger or providing clean water), and more.

Because people can experience different levels and internalizations of passion for different targets, we encourage researchers to be specific about the targets of passion in the individuals they study, and to allow for entrepreneurs to tell us what they are passionate about instead of presuming we know this already. This becomes especially important when we shift levels of analysis to focus on how the passions of individuals within founding teams converge or collide in terms of team passion diversity, or shift the referent to what the team itself is passionate about (team entrepreneurial passion, TEP) regardless of individual members' passions, which we discussed in Chapter 6.

While we spent some time in Chapter 4 talking about the potential profits and perils of entrepreneurial passion, and in Chapter 5 focusing on how passions can be ignited and stoked through action, training, and contagion pathways, there are many more questions that remain to be answered. Throughout each chapter, and especially in Chapter 7, we suggested numerous specific questions that remain and offered our recommendations for the conceptual and empirical precision needed for such work to build our collective knowledge about passion and entrepreneurs in a meaningful and rigorous way. In making a large number of suggestions for areas ripe for future inquiry throughout the book, we intentionally tried to create many "sparks" to see what "ignites" the fires of passion for this area of research in readers, to stoke those fires hotter for those already studying passion, and to bank the coals for those new to the area that may not yet be ready to jump into the flames.

Altogether, we hope we have provided a strong grounding in the current state of research concerning passion and entrepreneurship. We believe this book can serve as a meaningful reference point for ongoing research for both new and established academics. Yet, as we have noted previously, we do not consider our viewpoints and opinions to be the only veridical voices in this domain. Whenever possible, we try to engage others in fruitful debates about the construct of passion because we both believe that it is through engaged discourse that this body of knowledge moves closer to "truth." That is the spirit in which we have authored this book. We continue to be passionate about this area of research and hope that more scholars will join us in conducting research on this phenomenon in an effort to shed new light on how passion influences and is influenced by the process of entrepreneurship. We look forward to seeing what insights the next generation of research will yield.

References

Achievers.com. (2016). Top 5 best company mission statements. Retrieved from http://www.achievers.com/blog/top-5-best-company-mission-statements/ (last accessed 3/16/2020).

Adomdza, G. K., & Baron, R. A. (2013). The role of affective biasing in commercializing new ideas. *Journal of Small Business & Entrepreneurship, 26*(2), 201–217. doi:10.1080/08276331.2013.771864

Allison, T. H., Warnick, B. J., & Davis, B. C. (2018). *"It's not who you say – it's how you say it!": An audio content analysis of crowdfunding pitches.* Paper presented at the Babson College Entrepreneurship Research Conference, Waterford, Ireland.

Annies.com. (2015). About Annie's. Retrieved from http://www.annieshomegrown.ca/about-annies (last accessed 3/16/2020).

Ashforth, B. E., & Kreiner, G. E. (1999). "How can you do it?": Dirty work and the challenge of constructing a positive identity. *Academy of Management Review, 24*(3), 413–434. doi:10.5465/AMR.1999.2202129

Ashforth, B. E., & Mael, F. (1989). Social identity theory and the organization. *Academy of Management Review, 14*(1), 20–39. doi:10.5465/AMR.1989.4278999

Ashforth, B. E., Rogers, K. M., & Corley, K. G. (2011). Identity in organizations: Exploring cross-level dynamics. *Organization Science, 22*(5), 1144–1156. doi:10.1287/orsc.1100.0591

Audia, P. G., Locke, E. A., & Smith, K. G. (2000). The paradox of success: An archival and a laboratory study of strategic persistence following radical environmental change. *Academy of Management Journal, 43*(5), 837–853. doi:10.5465/1556413

Bandura, A. (1991). Social cognitive theory of self-regulation. *Organizational Behavior & Human Decision Processes, 50*(2), 248–287. doi:10.1016/0749-5978(91)90022-L

Bao, J., Zhou, X., & Chen, Y. (2017). Entrepreneurial passion and behaviors: Opportunity recognition as a mediator. *Social Behavior and Personality: An International Journal, 45*(7), 1211–1220. doi:http://dx.doi.org/10.2224/sbp.6492

Baron, R. A., & Henry, R. A. (2010). How entrepreneurs acquire the capacity to excel: Insights from research on expert performance. *Strategic Entrepreneurship Journal, 4*(1), 49–65. doi:10.1002/sej.82

Barsade, S. G., & Gibson, D. E. (1998). Group emotion: A view from top and bottom. In D. Gruenfeld, E. A. Mannix, & M. Neale (Eds.), *Research on Managing Groups and Teams* (pp. 81–102). Stamford, CT: JAI Press.

Barsade, S. G., & Gibson, D. E. (2012). Group affect: Its influence on individual and group outcomes. *Current Directions in Psychological Science, 21*(2), 119–123. doi:http://dx.doi.org/10.1177/0963721412438352

Barsade, S. G., Ward, A. J., Turner, J. D. R., & Sonnenfeld, J. A. (2000). To your heart's content: A model of affective diversity in top management teams. *Administrative Science Quarterly, 45*(4), 802–836. doi:10.2307/2667020

Bartel, C. A., & Saavedra, R. (2000). The collective construction of work group moods. *Administrative Science Quarterly, 45*(2), 197–231. doi:10.2307/2667070

Baum, J. R., & Locke, E. A. (2004). The relationship of entrepreneurial traits, skill, and motivation to subsequent venture growth. *Journal of Applied Psychology, 89*(4), 587–598. doi:10.1037/0021-9010.89.4.587

Bélanger, J. J., Schumpe, B. M., Nociti, N., Moyano, M., Dandeneau, S., Chamberland, P. E., & Vallerand, R. J. (2019). Passion and moral disengagement: Different pathways to political activism. *Journal of Personality, 87*(6), 1234–1249. doi:http://dx.doi.org/10.1111/jopy.12470

Black, G. (2019). *The Next Level Entrepreneur: Focus your Passions. Map Your Direction. Build a Great Company.* San Antonio, TX: Intigro Press, LLC.

Boone, S., Andries, P., & Clarysse, B. (in press). Does team entrepreneurial passion matter for relationship conflict and team performance? On the importance of fit between passion focus and venture development stage. *Journal of Business Venturing.* doi:10.1016/j.jbusvent.2019.105984

Breugst, N., Domurath, A., Patzelt, H., & Klaukien, A. (2012). Perceptions of entrepreneurial passion and employees' commitment to entrepreneurial ventures. *Entrepreneurship: Theory & Practice, 36*(1), 171–192. doi:10.1111/j.1540-6520.2011.00491.x

Brewer, M. B., & Gardner, W. (1996). Who is this "we"? Levels of collective identity and self representations. *Journal of Personality*

& Social Psychology, 71(1), 83–93. doi:10.1037/0022-3514.71.1.83

Burke, P. J. (1991). Identity processes and social stress. *American Sociological Review, 56*(6), 836–849. doi:http://dx.doi.org/10.2307/2096259

Burke, P. J. (2006). Identity change. *Social Psychology Quarterly, 69*(1), 81–96. doi:http://dx.doi.org/10.1177/019027250606900106

Campos, H. (2017). Impact of entrepreneurial passion on entrepreneurial orientation with the mediating role of entrepreneurial alertness for technology-based firms in Mexico. *Journal of Small Business and Enterprise Development, 24*(2), 353–374.

Carbonneau, N., Vallerand, R. J., Lavigne, G. L., & Paquet, Y. (2016). "I'm not the same person since I met you": The role of romantic passion in how people change when they get involved in a romantic relationship. *Motivation and Emotion, 40*(1), 101–117. doi:http://dx.doi.org/10.1007/s11031-015-9512-z

Cardon, M. S. (2008). Is passion contagious? The transference of entrepreneurial passion to employees. *Human Resource Management Review, 18*(2), 77–86. doi:10.1016/j.hrmr.2008.04.001

Cardon, M. S., & Kirk, C. P. (2015). Entrepreneurial passion as mediator of the self-efficacy to persistence relationship. *Entrepreneurship: Theory & Practice, 39*(5), 1027–1050. doi:10.1111/etap.12089

Cardon, M. S., Glauser, M., & Murnieks, C. Y. (2017a). Passion for what? Expanding the domains of entrepreneurial passion. *Journal of Business Venturing Insights, 8*, 24–32.

Cardon, M. S., Mitteness, C., & Sudek, R. (2017b). Motivational cues and angel investing: Interactions among enthusiasm, preparedness, and commitment. *Entrepreneurship: Theory & Practice, 41*(6), 1057–1085. doi:10.1111/etap.12255

Cardon, M. S., Post, C., & Forster, W. R. (2017c). Team entrepreneurial passion: Its emergence and influence in new venture teams. *Academy of Management Review, 42*(2), 283–305. doi:10.5465/amr.2014.0356

Cardon, M. S., Wincent, J., Singh, J., & Drnovsek, M. (2009). The nature and experience of entrepreneurial passion. *Academy of Management Review, 34*(3), 511–532. doi:10.5465/AMR.2009.40633190

Cardon, M. S., Gregoire, D. A., Stevens, C. E., & Patel, P. C. (2013). Measuring entrepreneurial passion: Conceptual foundations and scale validation. *Journal of Business Venturing, 28*(3), 373–396. doi:10.1016/j.jbusvent.2012.03.003

Cardon, M. S., Zietsma, C., Saparito, P., Matherne, B. P., & Davis, C. (2005). A tale of passion: New insights into entrepreneurship from a parenthood metaphor. *Journal of Business Venturing*, *20*(1), 23–45. doi:10.1016/j.jbusvent.2004.01.002

Chan, D. (1998). Functional relations among constructs in the same content domain at different levels of analysis: A typology of composition models. *Journal of Applied Psychology*, *83*(2), 234–246. doi:10.1037/0021-9010.83.2.234

Chen, C. C., Greene, P. G., & Crick, A. (1998). Does entrepreneurial self-efficacy distinguish entrepreneurs from managers? *Journal of Business Venturing*, *13*(4), 295–316. doi:10.1016/S0883-9026(97)00029-3

Chen, X.-P., Yao, X. I. N., & Kotha, S. (2009). Entrepreneur passion and preparedness in business plan presentations: A persuasion analysis of venture capitalists' funding decisions. *Academy of Management Journal*, *52*(1), 199–214. doi:10.5465/AMJ.2009.36462018

Chisholm, J. (2015). *Unleash your Inner Company: Use Passion and Perseverance to Build Your Ideal Business*. Austin, TX: Greenleaf Book Press Group.

Clarysse, B., Van Boxstael, A., & Van Hove, J. (2015). *A tale of two passions: A passion for the "profession" and a passion to "developing the venture."* Paper presented at the Academy of Management Annual Conference, Vancouver, British Columbia.

Cohen, D., Cardon, M. S., & Singh, J. (2019). *Anticipatory entrepreneurial passion and its dynamic role in shaping affect and effort of nascent entrepreneurs*. Paper presented at the Academy of Management Annual Conference, Boston, MA.

Collewaert, V., Anseel, F., Crommelinck, M., De Beuckelaer, A., & Vermeire, J. (2016). When passion fades: Disentangling the temporal dynamics of entrepreneurial passion for founding. *Journal of Management Studies*, *53*(6), 966–995. doi:10.1111/joms.12193

Conger, M., McMullen, J. S., Bergman, B. J., & York, J. G. (2018). Category membership, identity control, and the reevaluation of prosocial opportunities. *Journal of Business Venturing*, *33*(2), 179–206. doi:10.1016/j.jbusvent.2017.11.004

Curran, T., Hill, A. P., Appleton, P. R., Vallerand, R. J., & Standage, M. (2015). The psychology of passion: A meta-analytical review of a decade of research on intrapersonal outcomes. *Motivation and Emotion*, *39*(5), 631–655. doi:http://dx.doi.org/10.1007/s11031-015-9503-0

Dalborg, C., & Wincent, J. (2015). The idea is not enough: The role of self-efficacy in mediating the relationship between pull entrepreneurship and founder passion – a research note. *International Small Business Journal: Researching Entrepreneurship, 33*(8), 974–984. doi:10.1177/0266242614543336

Davidson, A. (2020). *The Passion Economy: Nine Rules for Thriving in the Twenty-first Century*. New York, NY: Random House LLC.

Davis, B. C., Hmieleski, K. M., Webb, J. W., & Coombs, J. E. (2017). Funders' positive affective reactions to entrepreneurs' crowdfunding pitches: The influence of perceived product creativity and entrepreneurial passion. *Journal of Business Venturing, 32*(1), 90–106. doi:10.1016/j.jbusvent.2016.10.006

de Jong, B. A., & Dirks, K. T. (2012). Beyond shared perceptions of trust and monitoring in teams: Implications of asymmetry and dissensus. *Journal of Applied Psychology, 97*(2), 391–406. doi:10.1037/a0026483

de Mol, E., Ho, V. T., & Pollack, J. M. (2018). Predicting entrepreneurial burnout in a moderated mediated model of job fit. *Journal of Small Business Management, 56*(3), 392–411. doi:10.1111/jsbm.12275

de Mol, E., Cardon, M. S., de Jong, B., Khapova, S., & Elfring, T. (in press). Entrepreneurial passion diversity in new venture teams: An empirical examination of short- and long-term performance implications. Journal of Business Venturing. doi:https://doi.org/10.1016/j.jbusvent.2019.105965

Deci, E. L., & Ryan, R. M. (1985). The general causality orientations scale: Self-determination in personality. *Journal of Research in Personality, 19*(2), 109–134. doi:http://dx.doi.org/10.1016/0092-6566(85)90023-6

DeRue, D. S., & Ashford, S. J. (2010). Who will lead and who will follow? A social process of leadership identity construction in organizations. *Academy of Management Review, 35*(4), 627–647. doi:10.5465/amr.35.4.zok627

Drnovsek, M., Cardon, M. S., & Patel, P. C. (2016). Direct and indirect effects of passion on growing technology ventures. *Strategic Entrepreneurship Journal, 10*(2), 194–213. doi:10.1002/sej.1213

Duckworth, A. L., Peterson, C., Matthews, M. D., & Kelly, D. R. (2007). Grit: Perseverance and passion for long-term goals. *Journal of Personality & Social Psychology, 92*(6), 1087–1101. doi:10.1037/0022-3514.92.6.1087

Dutton, J. E., Roberts, L. M., & Bednar, J. (2010). Pathways for positive identity construction at work: Four types of positive identity and the building of social resources. *Academy of Management Review, 35*(2), 265–293. doi:10.5465/amr.35.2.zok265

Ehrenberg, R. (2008). Monitor 100 – a post mortem. Retrieved from http://informationarbitrage.com/post/698402433/monitor110-a -post-mortem (last accessed 3/16/2020).

Fauchart, E., & Gruber, M. (2011). Darwinians, communitarians, and missionaries: The role of founder identity in entrepreneurship. *Academy of Management Journal, 54*(5), 935–957. doi:10.5465/ amj.2009.0211

Fisher, R., Merlot, E., & Johnson, L. W. (2018). The obsessive and harmonious nature of entrepreneurial passion. *International Journal of Entrepreneurial Behaviour and Research, 24*(1), 22–40.

Forbes, D. P. (2005). The effects of strategic decision making on entrepreneurial self-efficacy. *Entrepreneurship: Theory & Practice, 29*(5), 599–626. doi:10.1111/j.1540-6520.2005.00100.x

Gabrielle, G. (2017). *Turn your Passion into a Thriving Business – How to Start a Business that Will CRUSH it!!: A Rookie Entrepreneur Start-up Guide.* CreateSpace Independent Publishing Platform.

Gielnik, M. M., Uy, M. A., Funken, R., & Bischoff, K. M. (2017). Boosting and sustaining passion: A long-term perspective on the effects of entrepreneurship training. *Journal of Business Venturing, 32*(3), 334–353. doi:10.1016/j.jbusvent.2017.02.003

Gielnik, M. M., Spitzmuller, M., Schmitt, A., Klemann, D. K., & Frese, M. (2015). "I put in effort, therefore I am passionate": Investigating the path from effort to passion in entrepreneurship. *Academy of Management Journal, 58*(4), 1012–1031. doi:10 .5465/amj.2011.0727

Gimeno, J., Folta, T. B., Cooper, A. C., & Woo, C. Y. (1997). Survival of the fittest? Entrepreneurial human capital and the persistence of underperforming firms. *Administrative Science Quarterly, 42*(4), 750–783. doi:10.2307/2393656

Gioia, D. A., Patvardhan, S. D., Hamilton, A. L., & Corley, K. G. (2013). Organizational identity formation and change. *Academy of Management Annals, 7*(1), 123–193. doi:10.1080/19416520 .2013.762225

Glauser, M. (2009). *Entrepreneurial leadership: What success-ful entrepreneurs teach us about building thriving businesses.* Paper presented at the Society for Entrepreneurship Scholars Conference, Columbus, Ohio.

Griffio, I. (2019). *Mind Your Business: A Workbook to Grow Your Creative Passion into a Full-time Gig.* New York, NY: Paige Tate & Co.

Grimes, M. G. (2018). The pivot: How founders respond to feedback through idea and identity work. *Academy of Management Journal, 61*(5), 1692–1717. doi:10.5465/amj.2015.0823

Gross, J. J. (1999). Emotion regulation: Past, present, future. *Cognition & Emotion, 13*(5), 551–573. doi:10.1080/026999399379186

Gross, J. J. (2015). Emotion regulation: Current status and future prospects. *Psychological Inquiry, 26*(1), 1–26. doi:10.1080/1047840X.2014.940781

Guercini, S., & Ranfagni, S. (2016). Conviviality behavior in entrepreneurial communities and business networks. *Journal of Business Research, 69*(2), 770–776. doi:10.1016/j.jbusres.2015.07.013

Hamdi-Kidar, L., & Vellera, C. (2018). Triggers entrepreneurship among creative consumers. *Journal of Business Research, 92*, 465–473. doi:10.1016/j.jbusres.2018.07.018

Harrison, D. A., & Klein, K. J. (2007). What's the difference? Diversity constructs as separation, variety, or disparity in organizations. *Academy of Management Review, 32*(4), 1199–1228.

Hlady Rispal, M., & Servantie, V. (2017). Business models impacting social change in violent and poverty-stricken neighbourhoods: A case study in Colombia. *International Small Business Journal: Researching Entrepreneurship, 35*(4), 427–448.

Ho, V. T., & Pollack, J. M. (2014). Passion isn't always a good thing: Examining entrepreneurs' network centrality and financial performance with a Dualistic Model of Passion. *Journal of Management Studies, 51*(3), 433–459. doi:10.1111/joms.12062

Hollenbeck, J. R., & Klein, H. J. (1987). Goal commitment and the goal-setting process: Problems, prospects, and proposals for future research. *Journal of Applied Psychology, 72*(2), 212–220. doi:10.1037/0021-9010.72.2.212

Hsu, D. K., Simmons, S. A., & Wieland, A. M. (2017). Designing entrepreneurship experiments. *Organizational Research Methods, 20*(3), 379–412. doi:10.1177/1094428116685613

Huyghe, A., Knockaert, M., & Obschonka, M. (2016). Unraveling the "passion orchestra" in academia. *Journal of Business Venturing, 31*(3), 344–364. doi:10.1016/j.jbusvent.2016.03.002

Ibarra, H., & Barbulescu, R. (2010). Identity as narrative: Prevalence, effectiveness, and consequences of narrative identity work in macro work role transitions. *Academy of Management Review, 35*(1), 135–154. doi:10.5465/amr.35.1.zok135

Ibarra, H., & Petriglieri, J. L. (2010). Identity work and play. *Journal of Organizational Change Management, 23*(1), 10–25. doi:10.1108/09534811011017180

Jachimowicz, J. M., Wihler, A., Bailey, E. R., & Galinsky, A. D. (2018). *Why grit requires perseverance and passion to positively predict performance*. Paper presented at the National Academy of Sciences of the United States of America.

Jachimowicz, J. M., To, C., Agasi, S., Côté, S., & Galinsky, A. D. (2019). The gravitational pull of expressing passion: When and how expressing passion elicits status conferral and support from others. *Organizational Behavior & Human Decision Processes, 153*, 41–62. doi:10.1016/j.obhdp.2019.06.002

Kamm, J. B., Shuman, J. C., Seeger, J. A., & Nurick, A. J. (1990). Entrepreneurial teams in new venture creation: A research agenda. *Entrepreneurship: Theory & Practice, 14*(4), 7–17. doi:10.1177/104225879001400403

Kaplan, S., Luchman, J. N., Haynes, D., & Bradley, J. C. (2009). On the role of positive and negative affectivity in job performance: A meta-analytic investigation. *Journal of Applied Psychology, 94*(1), 162–176. doi:10.1037/a0013115

Klotz, A. C., Hmieleski, K. M., Bradley, B. H., & Busenitz, L. W. (2014). New venture teams: A review of the literature and roadmap for future research. *Journal of Management, 40*(1), 226–255. doi:10.1177/0149206313493325

Krieger, J. (2014). *Lifestyle Entrepreneur: Live Your Dreams, Ignite Your Passions and Run Your Business from Anywhere in the World*. Franklin, TN: Morgan James Publishing.

Kuratko, D. F., Hornsby, J. S., & Naffziger, D. W. (1997). An examination of owner's goals in sustaining entrepreneurship. *Journal of Small Business Management, 35*(1), 24–33.

Letwin, C., Stevenson, R., McKenney, A., & Cardon, M. S. (2016). *It's what you say, not just how you say it: The development of a passion dictionary and exploration into the effect of passionate rhetoric on funding outcomes*. Paper presented at the Babson College Entrepreneurship Research Conference, Bodo, Norway.

Li, J., Chen, X.-P., Kotha, S., & Fisher, G. (2017). Catching fire and spreading it: A glimpse into displayed entrepreneurial passion in crowdfunding campaigns. *Journal of Applied Psychology, 102*(7), 1075–1090. doi:10.1037/apl0000217

Lichtenstein, B. B., Carter, N. M., Dooley, K. J., & Gartner, W. B. (2007). Complexity dynamics of nascent entrepreneurship. *Journal of Business Venturing, 22*(2), 236–261. doi:10.1016/j.jbusvent.2006.06.001

Locke, E. A., & Latham, G. P. (1990). *A Theory of Goal-setting and Task Performance*. Englewood Cliffs, NJ: Prentice Hall.

Locke, E. A., & Latham, G. P. (2002). Building a practically useful theory of goal setting and task motivation. *American Psychologist, 57*(9), 705–717. doi:10.1037/0003-066X.57.9.705

Mageau, G. A., Carpentier, J., & Vallerand, R. J. (2011). The role of self-esteem contingencies in the distinction between obsessive and harmonious passion. *European Journal of Social Psychology, 41*(6), 720–729. doi:http://dx.doi.org/10.1002/ejsp.798

Mageau, G. A., Vallerand, R. J., Charest, J., Salvy, S.-J., Lacaille, N., Bouffard, T., & Koestner, R. (2009). On the development of harmonious and obsessive passion: The role of autonomy support, activity specialization, and identification with the activity. *Journal of Personality, 77*(3), 601–646. doi:http://dx.doi.org/10.1111/j.1467-6494.2009.00559.x

Markman, G. D., Baron, R. A., & Balkin, D. B. (2005). Are perseverance and self-efficacy costless? Assessing entrepreneurs' regretful thinking. *Journal of Organizational Behavior, 26*(1), 1–19. doi:10.1002/job.305

Markowska, M., Härtel, C. E. J., Brundin, E., & Roan, A. (2015). A dynamic model of entrepreneurial identification and dis-identification: An emotions perspective. In C. E. J. Härtel, W. J. Zerbe, & N. M. Ashkanasy (Eds.), *New Ways of Studying Emotions in Organizations* (pp. 215–239). Bingley: Emerald Group Publishing.

Martens, M. L., Jennings, J. E., & Jennings, P. D. (2007). Do the stories they tell get them the money they need? The role of entrepreneurial narratives in resource acquisition. *Academy of Management Journal, 50*(5), 1107–1132. doi:10.5465/AMJ.2007.27169488

Mathias, B. D., & Williams, D. W. (2018). Giving up the hats? Entrepreneurs' role transitions and venture growth. *Journal of Business Venturing, 33*(3), 261–277. doi:https://doi.org/10.1016/j.jbusvent.2017.12.007

McCall, G. J., & Simmons, J. L. (1966). A new measure of attitudinal opposition. *Public Opinion Quarterly, 30*(2), 271–278. doi:10.1086/267406

Mitteness, C., Sudek, R., & Cardon, M. S. (2012). Angel investor characteristics that determine whether perceived passion leads to higher evaluations of funding potential. *Journal of Business Venturing, 27*(5), 592–606. doi:10.1016/j.jbusvent.2011.11.003

Mueller, B. A., Wolfe, M. T., & Syed, I. (2017). Passion and grit: An exploration of the pathways leading to venture success. *Journal of Business Venturing, 32*(3), 260–279. doi:10.1016/j.jbusvent.2017.02.001

Murnieks, C. Y., & Cardon, M. S. (2019). Identities and passion at work. In R. J. Vallerand & N. Houlfort (Eds.), *Passion for Work: Determinants and Consequences* (pp. 67–104). New York, NY: Oxford University Press.

Murnieks, C. Y., Mosakowski, E., & Cardon, M. S. (2014). Pathways of passion: Identity centrality, passion, and behavior among entrepreneurs. *Journal of Management, 40*(6), 1583–1606. doi:10 .1177/0149206311433855

Murnieks, C. Y., Cardon, M. S., & Haynie, J. M. (2020). Fueling the fire: Examining identity centrality, affective interpersonal commitment and gender as drivers of entrepreneurial passion. *Journal of Business Venturing, 35*(1). doi:10.1016/j.jbusvent.2018.10.007

Murnieks, C. Y., Cardon, M. S., Sudek, R., White, T. D., & Brooks, W. T. (2016). Drawn to the fire: The role of passion, tenacity and inspirational leadership in angel investing. *Journal of Business Venturing, 31*(4), 468–484. doi:10.1016/j.jbusvent.2016.05.002

Naragon-Gainey, K., McMahon, T. P., & Chacko, T. P. (2017). The structure of common emotion regulation strategies: A meta-analytic examination. *Psychological Bulletin, 143*(4), 384–427. doi:10.1037/bul0000093

Newman, A., Obschonka, M., Moeller, J., & Chandan, G. G. (2019). Entrepreneurial passion: A review, synthesis, and agenda for future research. *Applied Psychology: An International Review.* doi:http://dx.doi.org/10.1111/apps.12236

Omorede, A., Thorgren, S., & Wincent, J. (2013). Obsessive passion, competence, and performance in a project management context. *International Journal of Project Management, 31*(6), 877–888. doi:10.1016/j.ijproman.2012.09.002

Oo, P. P., Allison, T. H., Sahaym, A., & Juasrikul, S. (2019). User entrepreneurs' multiple identities and crowdfunding performance: Effects through product innovativeness, perceived passion, and need similarity. *Journal of Business Venturing, 34*(5). doi:10 .1016/j.jbusvent.2018.08.005

Pollack, J. M., Ho, V. T., O'Boyle, E. H., & Kirkman, B. L. (in press). Passion at work: A meta-analysis of individual work outcomes. *Journal of Organizational Behavior.* doi:https://doi.org/10 .1002/job.2434

Powell, E. E., & Baker, T. E. D. (2014). It's what you make of it: Founder identity and enacting strategic responses to adversity. *Academy of Management Journal, 57*(5), 1406–1433. doi:10 .5465/amj.2012.0454

Powell, E. E., & Baker, T. E. D. (2017). In the beginning: Identity processes and organizing in multi-founder nascent ventures.

Academy of Management Journal, *60*(6), 2381–2414. doi:10.5465/amj.2015.0175

Pratt, M. G., Rockmann, K. W., & Kaufmann, J. B. (2006). Constructing professional identity: The role of work and identity learning cycles in the customization of identity among medical residents. *Academy of Management Journal*, *49*(2), 235–262. doi:10.5465/AMJ.2006.20786060

Pret, T., Cogen, A., & Cardon, M. S. (2020). *Live together and prosper: The process of household instrumental and emotional support of entrepreneurs* (currently under review).

Ratelle, C. F., Carbonneau, N., Vallerand, R. J., & Mageau, G. (2013). Passion in the romantic sphere: A look at relational outcomes. *Motivation and Emotion*, *37*(1), 106–120. doi:http://dx.doi.org/10.1007/s11031-012-9286-5

Rauch, A., & Frese, M. (2007). Let's put the person back into entrepreneurship research: A meta-analysis on the relationship between business owners' personality traits, business creation, and success. *European Journal of Work & Organizational Psychology*, *16*(4), 353–385. doi:10.1080/13594320701595438

Robb, A., & Reedy, E. J. (2012). *An overview of the Kauffman firm survey: Results from 2010 business activities*. Retrieved from SSRN: https://ssrn.com/abstract=2055265 (last accessed 3/16/2020).

Ruskin, J., Seymour, R. G., & Webster, C. M. (2016). Why create value for others? An exploration of social entrepreneurial motives. *Journal of Small Business Management*, *54*(4), 1015–1037. doi:10.1111/jsbm.12229

Ryan, R. M., & Deci, E. L. (2000). The darker and brighter sides of human existence: Basic psychological needs as a unifying concept. *Psychological Inquiry*, *11*(4), 319–338. doi:http://dx.doi.org/10.1207/S15327965PLI1104_03

Santos, S. C., & Cardon, M. S. (2019). What's love got to do with it? Team entrepreneurial passion and performance in new venture teams. *Entrepreneurship: Theory & Practice*, *43*(3), 475–504. doi:10.1177/1042258718812185

Sarasvathy, S. D. (2001). Causation and effectuation: Toward a theoretical shift from economic inevitability to entrepreneurial contingency. *Academy of Management Review*, *26*(2), 243–263. doi:10.5465/AMR.2001.4378020

Schellenberg, B. J. I., & Bailis, D. S. (2015). Can passion be polyamorous? The impact of having multiple passions on subjective well-being and momentary emotions. *Journal of Happiness Studies: An Interdisciplinary Forum on Subjective Well-Being*,

16(6),   1365–1381.   doi:http://dx.doi.org/10.1007/s10902-014
-9564-x

Schwarte, Y., Song, Y., & Hunt, R. (2019). *Entrepreneurial passion: Key dimensions and an integrative process model*. Paper presented at the Academy of Management Annual Conference, Boston, MA.

Schwarz, N., & Clore, G. L. (2007). Feelings and phenomenal experiences. In A. W. Kruglanski & E. T. Higgins (Eds.), *Social Psychology: Handbook of Basic Principles* (pp. 385–407). New York, NY: Guilford Press.

Seo, M.-G., Barrett, L. F., & Bartunek, J. M. (2004). The role of affective experience in work motivation. *The Academy of Management Review*, *29*(3), 423–439. doi:http://dx.doi.org/10.2307/20159052

Shepherd, D. A. (2003). Learning from business failure: Propositions of grief recovery for the self-employed. *Academy of Management Review*, *28*(2), 318–328. doi:10.5465/AMR.2003.9416377

Shepherd, D., & Haynie, J. M. (2009). Birds of a feather don't always flock together: Identity management in entrepreneurship. *Journal of Business Venturing*, *24*(4), 316–337. doi:10.1016/j.jbusvent .2007.10.005

Shepherd, D. A., & Zacharakis, A. (1999). Conjoint analysis: A new methodological approach for researching the decision policies of venture capitalists. *Venture Capital*, *1*(3), 197–217. doi:10.1080/ 136910699295866

Shepherd, D. A., Wiklund, J., & Haynie, J. M. (2009). Moving forward: Balancing the financial and emotional costs of business failure. *Journal of Business Venturing*, *24*(2), 134–148. doi:10 .1016/j.jbusvent.2007.10.002

Souitaris, V., Zerbinati, S., & Al-Laham, A. (2007). Do entrepreneurship programmes raise entrepreneurial intention of science and engineering students? The effect of learning, inspiration and resources. *Journal of Business Venturing*, *22*(4), 566–591. doi:10 .1016/j.jbusvent.2006.05.002

St-Louis, A. C., Carbonneau, N., & Vallerand, R. J. (2016). Passion for a cause: How it affects health and subjective well-being. *Journal of Personality*, *84*(3), 263–276. doi:http://dx.doi.org/10 .1111/jopy.12157

Stenholm, P., & Renko, M. (2016). Passionate bricoleurs and new venture survival. *Journal of Business Venturing*, *31*(5), 595–611. doi:10.1016/j.jbusvent.2016.05.004

Stock, R. M., Oliveira, P., & Hippel, E. (2015). Impacts of hedonic and utilitarian user motives on the innovativeness of user-developed

Solutions. *Journal of Product Innovation Management, 32*(3), 389–403. doi:10.1111/jpim.12201

Stroe, S., Parida, V., & Wincent, J. (2018). Effectuation or causation: An fsQCA analysis of entrepreneurial passion, risk perception, and self-efficacy. *Journal of Business Research, 89*, 265–272. doi: 10.1016/j.jbusres.2018.01.035

Stroe, S., Siren, C., Shepherd, D., & Wincent, J. (in press). The dualistic regulatory effect of passion on the relationship between fear of failure and negative affect: Insights from facial expression analysis. *Journal of Business Venturing.* doi:https://doi.org.10.1016/j.jbusvent.2019.105948

Stryker, S., & Burke, P. J. (2000). The past, present, and future of an identity theory. *Social Psychology Quarterly, 63*(4), 284–297. doi: http://dx.doi.org/10.2307/2695840

Sy, T., Côté, S., & Saavedra, R. (2005). The contagious leader: Impact of the leader's mood on the mood of group members, group affective tone, and group processes. *Journal of Applied Psychology, 90*(2), 295–305. doi:10.1037/0021-9010.90.2.295

Thorgren, S., & Wincent, J. (2013). Passion and challenging goals: Drawbacks of rushing into goal-setting processes. *Journal of Applied Social Psychology, 43*(11), 2318–2329. doi:10.1111/jasp.12181

Turner, T., & Gianiodis, P. (2018). Entrepreneurship unleashed: Understanding entrepreneurial education outside of the business school. *Journal of Small Business Management, 56*(1), 131–149. doi:10.1111/jsbm.12365

Vallerand, R. J. (2015). *The Psychology of Passion: A Dualistic Model.* New York, NY: Oxford University Press.

Vallerand, R. J., & Verner-Filion, J. (2013). Making people's life most worth living: On the importance of passion for positive psychology. *Terapia Psicológica, 31*(1), 35–48. doi:http://dx.doi.org/10.4067/S0718-48082013000100004

Vallerand, R. J., Paquet, Y., Philippe, F. L., & Charest, J. (2010). On the role of passion for work in burnout: A process model. *Journal of Personality, 78*(1), 289–312. doi:http://dx.doi.org/10.1111/j.1467-6494.2009.00616.x

Vallerand, R. J., Blanchard, C., Mageau, G. A., Koestner, R., Ratelle, C., Léonard, M., Gagné, M., & Marsolais, J. (2003). Les passions de l'âme: On obsessive and harmonious passion. *Journal of Personality & Social Psychology, 85*(4), 756–767. doi:10.1037/0022-3514.85.4.756

Warnick, B. J. (2014). *A tale of two passions: How non-entrepreneurial identities stimulate entrepreneurial activity.* Paper presented at the Academy of Management Annual Conference, Philadelphia, Pennsylvania.

Warnick, B. J., Murnieks, C. Y., McMullen, J. S., & Brooks, W. T. (2018). Passion for entrepreneurship or passion for the product? A conjoint analysis of angel and VC decision-making. *Journal of Business Venturing, 33*(3), 315–332. doi:10.1016/j.jbusvent.2018 .01.002

Weiss, H. M., & Cropanzano, R. (1996). Affective events theory: A theoretical discussion of the structure, causes and consequences of affective experiences at work. In B. M. Staw & L. L. Cummings (Eds.), *Research in Organizational Behavior* (Volume 18, Edition 1, pp. 1–74). Greenwich, CT: JAI Press.

Wennberg, K., Wiklund, J., DeTienne, D. R., & Cardon, M. S. (2010). Reconceptualizing entrepreneurial exit: Divergent exit routes and their drivers. *Journal of Business Venturing, 25*(4), 361–375. doi:10.1016/j.jbusvent.2009.01.001

Wu, C.-G., Gerlach, J. H., & Young, C. E. (2007). An empirical analysis of open source software developers' motivations and continuance intentions. *Information & Management, 44*(3), 253–262. doi:10.1016/j.im.2006.12.006

Zhao, H., & Seibert, S. E. (2006). The big five personality dimensions and entrepreneurial status: A meta-analytical review. *Journal of Applied Psychology, 91*(2), 259–271. doi:10.1037/0021-9010.91 .2.259

Zhao, H., Seibert, S. E., & Lumpkin, G. T. (2010). The relationship of personality to entrepreneurial intentions and performance: A meta-analytic review. *Journal of Management, 36*(2), 381–404. doi:10.1177/0149206309335187

Zigarmi, D., Nimon, K., Houson, D., Witt, D., & Diehl, J. (2009). Beyond engagement: Toward a framework and operational definition for employee work passion. *Human Resource Development Review, 8*(3), 300–326.